"It has been said that those who can, do and those who can't, teach. In his book, Mile One, Ed Roberts has mastered both and he shares his timeless principles, real world applications and invaluable insights with a truly rare level of authenticity. **It's not enough to be a great manager today - it takes true leadership to bring out the best in your team.** His book is a blueprint so I will be buying it for every one of my clients - and their managers!"

– David Spisak
CEO of Disruptive Growth Solutions
and The David Spisak Show Podcast

"Taking that first step with anything new can be a challenge. Thank you, Ed for giving us **Mile One**. This book will help others to start their journey."

– Larry C. Hourcle
Management Instructor
Academy National Automobile Dealers Association

"It's incredibly rare to find a book that so perfectly balances principle, practical application, and heart. This book has an abundance of all three. Ed's legacy of kind candor takes center stage as he opens his playbook — one that is changing both face of an industry and individuals alike. I repeatedly found myself inspired and longing to be a better leader, and I know you will too."

– Paul J Daly
Author
The Automotive Manifesto
and Founder of ASOTU

MILE ONE

AN ENDLESS JOURNEY TO EFFECTIVE LEADERSHIP

Ed Roberts

Daniel Gomez Enterprises, L.L.C.

Mile One: An Endless Journey to Effective Leadership
Copyright 2023, Ed Roberts
ISBN: 9798859680320
Hardcover

Published by Daniel Gomez Enterprises LLC /September 2023
Contact Info: (210) 663-5954 / Email: Info@DanielGomezGlobal.com

Dedication

This book is dedicated to the individual who forever changed the course of my life. It was on that fateful day, July 20, 1992, when you extended a much-needed lifeline of opportunity, reaching out to me when no one else would. Your belief in my potential set-in motion a journey that has shaped the very fabric of my existence today.

In the face of humble beginnings, you emerged as a guiding light, granting me my first job and igniting a fire within me that continues to burn bright to this day. When doors seemed closed and dreams appeared distant, you opened a door of possibilities and allowed me to step into a world of endless potential.

Your belief in me, when seemingly no one else would take a chance, has been a beacon of my inspiration. You saw beyond the surface, recognizing the determination and hunger for success that resided within me. Your simple act of kindness has resonated deeply within me, reminding me of the incredible power one individual holds to transform the course of another's life.

Through your guidance, you not only provided me with a job, but you instilled within me a sense of purpose, resilience, determination, and self-belief. Your example taught me the importance of lifting others up, fostering an environment of growth and empowerment, and recognizing the intrinsic potential that lies within every individual.

As I reflect on my journey and the accomplishments I have achieved, I am keenly aware that I would not be where I am today without your unwavering support and the chance you gave me. This book stands as a testament to the lessons you imparted, and the determination you ignited.

By dedicating this book to you, Charlie Waters, I hope to honor the remarkable impact you have had on my life and inspire countless others to believe in their own potential, embrace opportunities with courage, and extend a helping hand to those in need. Your simple act of kindness has created a ripple effect of positive change, and it is my mission to pay forward the same spirit of generosity you showed me.

With profound gratitude,

Ed Roberts

Table of Contents

Acknowledgements   *p. i*

Foreword by Letti Bozard   *p. v*

Introduction   *p. vii*

Chapter 1
The Journey   *p. 1*

Chapter 2
Be Visible   *p. 13*

Chapter 3
Busy vs Effective   *p. 23*

Chapter 4
Counseling vs Coaching   *p. 33*

Chapter 5
Perception vs Reality   *p. 43*

Chapter 6
Motivation vs Inspiration   *p. 55*

Chapter 7
Trust   *p. 65*

Chapter 8
Collaboration   *p. 75*

Chapter 9
Memories   *p. 85*

Chapter 10
Leveraging Strengths   *p. 95*

Chapter 11
Hire to Compliment   *p. 105*

Chapter 12
Team Building   *p. 115*

Chapter 13
Who Needs a Title   *p. 125*

Chapter 14
Tying It All Together   *p. 137*

Conclusion   *p. 151*

About the Author   *p. 155*

Acknowledgments

I would like to express my heartfelt gratitude to the outstanding individuals who have had a profound impact on my leadership journey and supported me along the way. Your unwavering belief, guidance, and trust have been instrumental in shaping my path to success.

Emily Roberts, my beloved daughter, you are my purpose and inspiration. Your presence in my life has taught me the true meaning of love, leadership, and responsibility. I am immensely proud of the clever and strategic decisions you have made and the person you are becoming. I am proud to be your dad, and I am even more proud to call you, my daughter.

Natasha Fay, the love of my life, your unwavering support and belief in my dreams have been my constant motivation. Thank you for always promoting and encouraging me to strive for greatness. I genuinely enjoy every moment we spend together on our journey through life. Natasha, you are everything that I am not, and that is one of the many things that will continue to make us stronger together.

Don Cisler, a man who took on the role of my father and became the grandfather figure to Emily without any blood ties, thank you for your unconditional love, support, and the invaluable life lessons you have imparted. Your presence in our lives has been truly transformative.

Todd Irish, my dearest friend, thank you for always pushing me to surpass my limits. Whether we talk every day or not, your support and encouragement have been a constant source of motivation. You are the epitome of what a best friend should be. Your unwavering belief in my potential has fueled my ambition and drive to achieve more. You are a true inspiration to many.

Esther Gibson, the mother of Emily, I am grateful for your commitment to co-parenting with me, keeping our daughter at the center of focus and the ease with which we have collaborated. Your support and understanding have made our journey as co-parents a near seamless one. She certainly turned out pretty remarkable!

Crystal Garrison, for being an exceptional colleague, assistant, and a true source of inspiration. Your trust in me to be your professional mentor and your dedication to excellence and high performance in all roles have been nothing short of amazing. Your growth and development as a professional have been unwavering, and I am honored to have played a role in your journey.

Mike Shad, my lifelong business mentor, your wisdom and exemplary approach to business have been instrumental in my growth. Your guidance and role modeling have shaped my professional journey and taught me valuable lessons.

Bo and Letti Bozard, the visionary sibling owners of Bozard Ford Lincoln, I am grateful for the opportunities you have provided me. Your forward-thinking mindset and love of people is unmatched for any industry. Your trust and willingness to let me try new things have been the foundation of my career growth.

Grace Looney, it is an absolute honor to continue to watch you grow both personally and professionally. Your creative mind, attention to detail, and the bravery to take on the challenge of creating Bozard University, which provides our team members with the best opportunities to develop their full potential. Your dedication to their growth is commendable and has made and continues to make a significant impact on our organization.

Jeff King, thank you for consistently challenging me to think bigger and outside of the box. Your guidance and push for excellence have shaped my leadership style and helped me grow in unimaginable ways.

John Fillare, your entertaining personality is second to none. Thank you for allowing me to constantly challenge you to surpass your own limitations. Your growth and determination to exceed your own expectations have been commendable.

Ron Overs, thank you for inspiring me to share my story with the automotive world and providing the guidance I needed to feel confident in doing so.

Clint Pulver, your inspiration, and encouragement were the catalysts that finally pushed me to pen this book. Thank you for igniting my passion and reminding me of the impact I can make.

To my entire team at Bozard Ford Lincoln, your trust in me as your leader has been and continues to be humbling. Thank you for your dedication, hard work, and for consistently giving your best.

Lastly, I would like to express my gratitude to all those whose names are not mentioned here but have touched my life in profound ways. Your support, encouragement, and belief in me have been invaluable.

This book would not be possible without all of you, the impactful individuals who have shaped my leadership journey. Thank you for being a part of my life and for inspiring me to strive for greatness.

Foreword

As Ed Roberts asked me to write the foreword to his first book, I could not help but liken the last two decades to an epic road trip. There have been backroads and breakdowns, fog-filled high beams, and high-speed highways. A trip where every sharp curve opens to a beautiful view. Over time, more cars have been added to the caravan, but we are still on the gas (Especially Ed!) and looking at each day as if it were just *Mile One*.

Ed and I have both worked in the same industry for all our careers, the last 15 years being on the same team. Both of our roles have evolved and grown, but always intertwined. We simultaneously set goals that would require us to develop ourselves into leaders of highly productive teams. I can say without any hesitation that no person, class, book, or seminar has impacted my personal leadership journey more than learning with and from Ed Roberts. He embodies intentionality. He learns from his mistakes. He creates actionable plans. He empowers others. And, my favorite trait, he never forgets to offer a hand up to those in whom he sees a glimpse of his own story.

Ed has lived the phrase "Life is about the journey, not the destination." I have had a window seat to his creation and implementation of the *Mile One* philosophy. He has lived it, adapted it, and continues to perfect it every day in our company's operations. And in this book, he selflessly shares it with all of us. Many of the strategies in *Mile One* cost no money but they do require investment. They are simple but they are not easy. With the right attitude and effort, they are likely the exact game changers you have been searching for.

I am profoundly grateful to Ed for his impact on the trajectory of our company and on me personally. Professionally, I am excited for everyone in every industry to have a book like *Mile One* to guide them toward their greatest success. Personally, I am proud of my friend for sharing his heart with the world.

Letti Bozard

Bozard Ford Lincoln

Introduction

Welcome to *Mile One: An Endless Journey to Effective Leadership*, a book born from my decades-long odyssey in the dynamic and ever-evolving landscape of the retail automotive industry. Throughout my thirty-plus year expedition, I have navigated countless challenges, embraced transformative experiences, and gleaned valuable insights on the art of leadership. It is with great enthusiasm and gratitude that I share these lessons with you, as together we embark on a relentless pursuit of effective leadership.

Leadership is not a destination but a continuous voyage, a perpetual journey of growth, self-discovery, and influence. Whether you are a seasoned pro, long term executive, a startup founder, or an aspiring leader, this book is for you. It is designed to provide valuable insights, practical strategies, and thought-provoking reflections that will elevate your leadership skills to new heights.

In this book, I invite you to join me on a transformative voyage, one that transcends the notion of a linear path and embraces the concept of *Mile Ones*. These *Mile Ones* represent the crucial junctures where we break down our overarching vision into tangible and achievable steps. As each *Mile One* is conquered, it becomes the foundation for the next milestone, propelling us forward in our leadership journey. Effective leadership is not just about managing the day-to-day minutia, it is about shaping habits and behaviors of ourselves and our team to be the envy of your industry. Afterall, someone has to be #1, why can't that be you?

Within these pages, we will delve into a diverse range of topics essential to effective leadership. From the importance of visibility and understanding the delicate balance between busyness and effectiveness, to the nuanced dynamics of counseling versus coaching and perception versus reality, we will explore the depths of these concepts and how they shape our leadership approach.

Additionally, we will uncover the power of motivation versus inspiration, the indispensable role of trust and collaboration, and the art of creating memorable moments that leave an indelible impact. Furthermore, we will explore the art of delegation through leveraging strengths, the strategic approach to hiring that leads to victory, and the profound significance of team building. We will challenge the notion that a title is a prerequisite for leadership, unlocking the understanding that true leadership knows no boundaries. Finally, in the closing chapter, we will wrap up with the art of navigating change in a positive and productive way.

At the end of each chapter, you will find three reflection questions designed to deepen your understanding, provoke introspection, and encourage practical application of the chapter's content. These questions are intended to guide your personal exploration, helping you connect the concepts to your own experiences and foster meaningful growth as a leader.

I am humbled and honored to share the valuable insights and hard-earned wisdom from my ongoing leadership journey. My hope is that *Mile One* serves as a guiding light, igniting your passion for effective leadership and empowering you to embrace each milestone with purpose and determination. Together, let us embark on this endless journey, where the pursuit of excellence knows no bounds and the transformative power of leadership awaits us at every turn. Together, we will discover the transformative power of leadership and empower ourselves to make a lasting difference in the lives of others.

Let the journey begin!

Chapter 1

The Journey

In the dimly lit corner of an automobile dealership, where the aroma of engine oil lingered in the air, a young man embarked on an extraordinary journey that would forever shape his perspective on leadership. This is where my story began, as an apprentice technician, with a past overshadowed by homelessness and adversity. The world had seemingly turned its back on me, leaving me with nothing but determination and a burning desire to prove myself.

Days and nights blurred together as I fought tooth and nail to survive. Mowing lawns, sifting through dumpsters for recyclables such as glass bottles, cardboard, and aluminum cans. I did whatever it took to scrape by. Rejection became my constant companion, each closed door fueling the fire within me. Yet, amid the struggle, a flicker of hope remained, guiding me toward a path that would transform my life and the lives of others.

When I finally secured a job at that dealership, I found myself facing a seemingly insurmountable challenge. I had no formal training, no expertise to rely on, and the weight of expectations bore down upon me. Every task felt like an uphill battle, an overwhelming mountain to climb. It was in this crucible of uncertainty that the essence of *Mile One* was born, a philosophy that would become my guiding light.

I realized that if I could break down each task, each responsibility into manageable steps, they became attainable. By simplifying complex goals and visions into actionable items, I discovered the power of *Mile One*, my next step, the next mile on the endless journey to effective leadership. Though I did not yet have a name for this approach, its impact was undeniable. *Mile One* became the catalyst for my personal transformation, as I proved time and again that with the right mindset and perseverance, anything could be achieved.

As I grew professionally, ascending the ranks and leading teams, I witnessed the transformative power of *Mile One* in the lives of others. By helping my team members break down their responsibilities into smaller, achievable components, I empowered them to see the once-daunting tasks as conquerable challenges. I became known as a leader who offered a helping hand, who believed in the potential of every individual. *Mile One* had evolved into more than a personal mantra, it had become a philosophy of leadership, a way of life.

Today, I stand as a highly respected leader, humbled by my journey and committed to sharing the lessons I learned along the way. *Mile One* serves as a reminder that no matter where we start, with persistence, dedication, and a willingness to help others, we can embark on an endless journey to effective leadership. Join me as we explore the transformative power of breaking things down, step by step, to unlock our full potential and achieve greatness together.

In the world we live in today, we frequently get caught up

"I realized that if I could break down each task, each responsibility into manageable steps, they became attainable."

with all the things competing for our time and attention. Then we do not end up concentrating on very many, or any at all. In reference to this book, I want to look at it mostly from a business standpoint. We have the endless count of key performance indicators (KPI's) that need our attention, the personnel concerns that arise, the needed processes that would drive efficiencies, the constant revamping of marketing strategies, the challenges of staying current with the changing market conditions. We all know the list is endless.

When we reflect on these things, it is like looking at an endless staircase, with each step being something we need to work on. The truth is, we cannot work on every step at once, we cannot step on the top step before we travel up the staircase. This is where we must intentionally prioritize the order of what we truly need to work on next, and then the next one after that, and so on. I am not saying you need to be the one that does all of it, but you do need to be involved with at least determining who needs to work on that next step. The more you delegate determines how many steps you can truly work on at the same time. We will elaborate more on delegation in a later chapter.

The next step is not the entire staircase, it is the entire staircase broken down into manageable steps, steps that will get you and your team to the desired goals. The goal is the big picture, and taking steps to get there makes it manageable, and achievable to you and your team. Steps can be slightly modified or completely changed along the way as needed with unexpected or uncontrollable changes to supply chains, market conditions, customer demands, just to name a few disruptors. With this flexibility, we become adaptable, and nimbler as needed when needed.

So, on my journey of leading teams effectively, I have found it remarkably effective to put it into the terms of traveling along an endless journey. We have all heard the famous phrase, "You cannot travel a journey of a thousand miles until you take that first step." Well, we cannot travel any part of that endless journey without traveling the first mile, then the next mile, then the next mile after that one, and so on. One of the things I ask my team frequently is what is your next *Mile One*? That next mile is always their *Mile One*, that mile one is their next step or action for that moment or day. What I am really asking them is, have you thought about and planned your next move? This requires intentionality, and with intentionality we are shifting our mind into the needed action to accomplish that next *Mile One*.

Often, we come in every day to work on whatever lands in our lap. When we do this, we are not usually very effective, because we are reacting to the situations that come up throughout the day-to-day business. This puts us in a situation where we are working in the business and not working on the business. When we are working on the business, we are doing the necessary things to stay ahead of the changing market conditions, looking for new strategies to challenge the status quo, developing our teams, or other meaningful opportunities to help elevate our business. When we are working in the business, we are just trying to keep things going as they are, hanging onto or keeping things in place that may not be as effective or efficient as they need to be in the current conditions.

If we continue to work in the business, we will rarely make progress because we will be consumed with extinguishing the current flames, or in our minds, we are doing whatever it is to prevent that flame from exploding into something uncontrollable.

To put it bluntly, if you do not have a plan for the day, the day will have a plan for you. So, it is important to start every day

"To put it bluntly, if you do not have a plan for the day, the day will have a plan for you."

with a plan with a significant level of commitment. However, there will be things that arise that require all hands-on deck, obviously you should tend to urgent matters. In those scenarios, you may have to re-prioritize your plan and have a new next *Mile One*. I caution you to be very intentional with what you deem urgent when you are reprioritizing.

Digesting this, what is your next *Mile One*? Reflect on how things are going and determine the next most important action you and your team need to act on. Now that you are intentionally thinking about your next step, let's think about the top three, what are the next three things you need to work on? Now we have three steps that we need to prioritize in order of which one is first, second, third. That first one, now becomes your next *Mile One*. Then as you manage, address, or conquer that next step, the second one becomes your next *Mile One*.

Mile One is the next thing that you need to work on. We need to work on this list every day, then if the day takes over and pulls us away, we now already have a plan for tomorrow. Let's be honest, the day does not usually take over. We react to the situation at hand, then find something else to react to, and we do this over and over throughout the day and allow menial tasks to prevent us from making progress and attending to our next *Mile One*. Now that we know what our next *Mile One* entails, we can begin to focus on it.

We need to be intentional with our teams to help them learn how to plan out their days as well. If they are front-line, there will be obstacles that will arise during the normal activity of business that will require their immediate attention. Then, commonly they will have to push their *Mile One* off for a bit. It is our responsibility to make sure they are creating their next *Mile One*, and to help them learn how to prioritize them. When our people have clear expectations and understand how to prioritize, it is less likely for them to feel overwhelmed because they know where to start! As they complete their next *Mile One*, they will feel a sense of accomplishment as it will break up their routine of doing the same thing repeatedly.

What is your next *Mile One?* We all have those days that we come in, and it seems like it is one thing after another, and at the end of the day, we feel like we did not get anything done. Yes, we all have those days. But if we have our next *Mile One* in mind, then just before we wrap up the day, we focus on it for a few minutes, and miraculously we conquer it, then we suddenly get a sense of accomplishment, and we do not feel like the day was a waste. This is the perfect time to prepare for your next *Mile One*, and overtime, you will amaze yourself and your team with all the progress you and your team are regularly making.

I will give you another example of having your next few mile ones. When you interviewed for the role you are in now, somewhere along the way you may have asked, or the hiring manager may have stated the reason they are looking for someone new is because the previous person did not focus on these three to five things. As soon as you hear those things, you think, *I can make that happen, that is right in my wheelhouse.* Those are the things that become the low-hanging fruit that you get the opportunity to make an impact on as soon as you get going in your new role. That is your next *Mile One*, and the next, and so on. The truth is, those three to five things always exist, we just need to identify them and prioritize the order we are going to work on them. The reason those things always exist is, we are truly on a journey, and on this journey we never arrive. We will always have our next *Mile One* if we intentionally look for it.

Lastly, I will give you an actual example of one of my team members, JJ, looking at what he thought was an insurmountable task. Our organization was growing, and he needed to figure out how he was going to add another warehouse to the two he was already managing. I would frequently ask him how his preparation was going, his response was usually, "I don't know how I'm going to do this boss; this may actually be too much on me." I let this go for some time, hoping at some point he would see the light. As the project started coming together and we had a clear deadline for completion. To this point JJ had not started preparation for the additional warehouse. It was time to step in. I sat down with JJ to have the *Mile One* conversation with him.

Together, we made a list of everything we could think of that needed to take place before we opened. We then determined a solid timeline and organized each of the things that needed to happen beforehand. With sixty-four items that required his attention, we determined that he would need to conquer at least four of them per week until all of them were completed. By knowing and prioritizing each of the tasks, he could then delegate them, or handle them himself. Almost in an instant, the task that he originally felt was insurmountable was now reasonable, and it happened nearly seamlessly.

Now as I pass by this same team member today, I frequently ask him and others in passing, "What is your next *Mile One*?" We all need this reminder to keep us focused on today's opportunities, and our opportunities of tomorrow. So, my first challenge for you from this book is, what is your next *Mile One*, and what is the next *Mile One* for each of your team members? It is important to know what their next *Mile One* entails, so you can be there to offer the guidance they may need to keep them growing, developing, and prioritizing their next *Mile One*.

Reflecting on "The Journey"

1. Are you currently prioritizing your tasks and responsibilities effectively, or are you getting caught up in reacting to day-to-day situations? Reflect on your approach to task management and consider how intentional prioritization can help you make progress towards your goals.

_____

_____

_____

_____

2. What is your next _Mile One_ in your professional journey? Take a moment to identify a specific goal or action that you can focus on to move forward.

_____

_____

_____

_____

3. How can you promote intentional planning and prioritization within your team? Reflect on ways you can help your team members identify their own _Mile One_ and prioritize their tasks effectively. Consider the impact this can have on their sense of accomplishment and overall productivity.

_____

_____

_____

_____

Notes

Chapter 2

Be Visible

In the realm of leadership, the power of visibility cannot be overstated. As leaders, it is not enough to simply set expectations and hope for the best. We must actively engage with our teams and be present in their daily endeavors. Being visible means more than physically occupying space, it encompasses fostering connections, building relationships, and catching our team members doing what we hired them to do. This chapter explores the profound impact of being visible as a leader, shedding light on the importance of genuine presence, recognition, and the transformative potential it holds. By embracing the art of visibility, we create an environment that inspires trust, motivates excellence, and nurtures a culture where every individual feels seen, valued, and empowered to reach their full potential.

One thing I like to do is catch people working. Actually, it is more of catching them doing what we hired them to do. When we catch them in their element, it gives us the opportunity to compliment them on the job they are doing. It also gives us an opportunity to stop and take notice of what they are doing and see if we can offer guidance along the way.

"By embracing the art of visibility, we create an environment that inspires trust, motivates excellence, and nurtures a culture where every individual feels seen, valued, and empowered to reach their full potential."

I use the phrase, "I want to catch people working," frequently. There are so many things we can get from this. I also add to that phrase that what you catch someone doing something three times in a row, that is most likely what they are doing most of the time. Let me elaborate on this a little bit more. Sometimes we have made that great hire and we think they are plug and play. Sometimes they are, and sometimes they are the previous employer's worst nightmare. If you are making yourself visible, you could also be setting the tone for what should be accomplished. Additionally, making yourself visible also gives you the opportunity to catch people working or catch them doing things that they should or should not be doing.

I will give you an example. If you catch Tim gathering people over to create a conversation about something, or laughing about something in the warehouse or in a setting that pulls people together, first, we need to try to figure out what is going on. Sometimes it may be productive, but more times than not it is counterproductive. Then not only is that person not being productive, but everyone that he can pull into his circle is not being productive either.

The one thing that I want you to notice is, if you are out and about being able to notice what people are doing, then you are most likely being effective and not too busy being caught up in your day-to-day minutia. We will spend a little more time on busy versus effective in the next chapter.

If you are out and about amongst your team, it sets a whole different tone for everyone involved. If your team can expect you to be in their space at a moment's notice, they are more apt to stay on task. They want you to catch them working! Have you ever heard the phrase "the tail wags the dog"? This

"...if you are out and about being able to notice what people are doing, then you are most likely being effective and not too busy being caught up in your day-to-day minutia."

will happen more than you think if you are not visible. Most will appreciate your presence, allowing them to become more comfortable with you, in turn making you more approachable. Some will look for the opportunity to catch you not looking and be the disruptor. To be effective at this, you cannot be in a routine doing the same thing at the same time every single day. Make your presence known, go out and talk to your people at various times of the day, and have different content that you are asking about.

Now, while you are trying to catch people working, you are also making connections, and sometimes while you are making connections you can figure out what they are struggling with. Notice everything that I have said so far. You must be intentional about catching your team working and setting the stage to connect with them. If you are being intentional about catching people working or catching them doing what they do on a normal basis, then you will learn what they need in order to grow, and whether you need to keep them on task with certain things. Catching them in their natural element allows you to notice coaching opportunities and promotes further development. What you are truly doing is setting the tone for what is expected of them.

All too often we hire people, we plug them into their role that we needed them to fill, then we leave them alone to either survive, die, or even worse, become the disruptor that you were warned about when you checked their reference. The fact is, we did not do a particularly good job of training and setting clear expectations, so they go out and they try to keep themselves busy. Usually, not even doing anything remotely close to what we expected them to do. We find them totally off task and no one to blame but ourselves, because we did not set expectations. This again is highlighted when you are trying to catch them working.

Now that you are catching them working, you have the opportunity to catch them doing the next right thing, or going above and beyond, or helping the person next to them, and so on. You may find they are doing additional research to better prepare themselves for what is ahead. They are keeping things organized in a way that helps them be more efficient and effective. This is the time when you catch people doing something right. When you catch them doing something right, now is the time to make sure they know you caught them! This is when you get the opportunity to make a big deal about it, you can tell them that you saw them doing whatever action it was, and that you appreciate them and that it is exactly what makes them a great part of the team. Let's not stop there. Take that a step further and talk about it in staff meetings and allow the drive-bys to begin! We will touch more on drive-bys in a later chapter. This will encourage others to go see them and thank them for their contributions. In our organization we refer to these moments as "bright spots" and we share them as often as possible!

This lets them know that you are truly taking notice of things they are doing both right and maybe not so right and when you make a big deal of the things they are doing right, they will always want to repeat that for which they get recognized or praised. So, are you recognizing and praising them enough?

Notice that we started with catching our teams being on task, but in turn, it led to us catching them doing things above and beyond, as well as identifying areas of opportunities for them to grow both personally and professionally all while connecting with them as a person. When we are connecting with them, they are, in turn, connecting with you. This sets the stage for ongoing open communication from both sides so you can learn why they do what they do and for whom they do it. The why they do what they do is their purpose, and it is important to know their purpose to truly connect with them.

In closing, let's remember that being visible as a leader is not an act of mere observation, but rather an intentional and initiative-taking engagement with our team members. By being present, attentive, and actively catching our team members doing what we hired them to do, we foster an environment where individuals are empowered, growth is nurtured, and collective success becomes the norm. So, let us embark on the transformative journey of visibility, knowing that our presence has the power to inspire greatness, build connections, and shape the destiny of our teams. As leaders, let's embrace the art of being visible and witness firsthand the extraordinary impact it has on our organizations, our people, and ourselves. Remember, leadership is not just about catching people working; it is about creating an environment where individuals thrive, grow, develop, and feel valued.

Reflecting on "Be Visible"

1. How often do you intentionally make yourself visible and catch your team members working? Reflect on the impact this visibility can have on setting the tone and keeping individuals on task. Consider how you can incorporate this practice into your leadership approach.

_____

_____

_____

_____

2. Are you effectively connecting with your team members while catching them working? Take a moment to assess whether you are using these opportunities to make meaningful connections and identify areas for growth. Reflect on how you can improve your approach to coaching and supporting your team members.

_____

_____

_____

_____

3. Do you praise and recognize your team members enough for their achievements and contributions? Consider the importance of acknowledging and celebrating their efforts, both individually and in group settings. Reflect on ways you can enhance your recognition practices to motivate and encourage your team members further.

_____

_____

_____

_____

Notes

Chapter 3

Busy vs. Effective

In our fast-paced and demanding world, it is all too easy to fall into the trap of being busy without being truly effective. Being busy implies a constant state of activity, a flurry of tasks and responsibilities that consume our time and energy. It gives us the illusion of productivity, as we rush from one item on our to-do list to the next. However, true effectiveness goes beyond mere busyness. It is about achieving meaningful outcomes, making a lasting impact, and prioritizing tasks that align with our goals and values. Effectiveness requires clarity, focus, and strategic thinking, allowing us to discern the vital few from the trivial many. In this chapter, we delve into the thought-provoking differences between being busy and being effective, unraveling the factors that contribute to each and exploring practical strategies to shift from a state of busyness to one of authentic effectiveness. Prepare to challenge the status quo, redefine your approach to productivity, and discover the transformative power of being truly effective in your leadership journey.

All too often we find ourselves saying, "I have been so busy I have not had time to do anything today." Without a doubt, in the time we live in, we do live very busy lives. With that said,

"Effectiveness requires clarity, focus, and strategic thinking, allowing us to discern the vital few from the trivial many."

the busy lives that we live at work is usually just that, busy. We make ourselves busy picking up things that need to be completed, but more times than not we are doing things that keep us busy, and yes, busy is rarely effective. We pick up things that we know we can do relatively quickly. We feel like we can handle this for someone on our team and we justify it in our minds with, "If I take it from them, they will be able to get something else done," so we tell ourselves we are helping our teams be more productive. We find ways to convince ourselves that it is the right thing to do. Over time, as we take things off their plate that we know we can handle fairly quick, we find ourselves with more and more to do every single day, instead of helping our teams learn how to overcome the roadblock that stopped them in the beginning. We enable the behavior and justify to ourselves "I can just do it, that's what I used to do, I'm good at it, and it will just be quicker if I do it anyway."

Let's look at an example we all have most likely experienced. How many times have you been to lunch, or just left for the day, or on vacation, or in a meeting and your phone is blowing up because someone on your team needs support. Yes, we need to be there for that support, but once you understand the scenario, you find that they did not really need you, that they could have made the decision and kept things moving without you. We must look at ourselves for that because we did not empower them, train them, or develop their level of confidence, therefore you become their only resource. They feel like they cannot do anything without you, in turn, you become very busy. News flash, that is exactly what you taught them!

Let's dive a bit deeper into what that really does to our team. When we make ourselves busy, we do not have time to go out and connect with our people. We do not have time to develop our people. We do not have time to plan for tomorrow. We do not have time to create a real meaningful plan for our business. We do not have time to make the deposits that we need to make with our people to help them grow and assure them that we genuinely care about them. We do not have time to let them know that they play a vital role in our organization. We do not have time to hire the right candidate, we hire the next candidate instead. We hire the convenient one instead of searching and finding the right candidate that can actually compliment the team. We become reactive to almost everything we do. This probably sounds familiar! The truth is, in most cases, we started doing this to ourselves on day one after moving into our current role, and we never got going in the right direction because we made ourselves busy and not highly effective.

Let us look at it from a different angle for a moment. If we stop taking those things that make us busy away from our team, and start showing them how to do them, several things start to happen. Unfortunately, we do not do this simply because we feel like they are too busy, or we tell ourselves, "We are the best one to do that particular task anyway," so you think, *I will just handle it for them*. What we are really telling them without saying it is, "I do not think you can manage that very well, so I will just do it for you."

On the other hand, when they come to us to let us know they are at an impasse with something, we now have all kinds of opportunities in front of us. If we show them how to do it, we let them know that we want them to grow and that we have the confidence in them that they can do it just as well as you can. When we do these things, it makes our people less dependent on us and they start to feel empowered to do it, rather than waiting for you. When they feel empowered, they will keep the ball rolling and without hesitation, they will start doing the next right thing.

Let's take a deeper look at what we now have time for as we guide our team rather than take stuff from them. We now have time to slow down the hiring process, and interview multiple people, in-turn giving us a better chance to make a choice of which candidate, rather than the only one that we interviewed.

You now have the time to work *on* your business rather than work *in* your business. When you work on your business you are finding new opportunities, new things to try, things that may actually challenge the status quo and truly set you and your business apart.

There are so many factors that come from developing our people to do the things that allow them to grow in their roles. We have only mentioned a few thus far. It is worth mentioning that when we are developing our people to do the elements of their current job or some of the elements of the roles that we are preparing them for, or that they may be seeking, their confidence starts to soar. Then they start looking to pick up new responsibilities because they want to grow as well. Confidence is paramount to making your team less dependent on you.

These are different forms of making deposits with our team so that they grow both personally and professionally. When we help them gain confidence and empower them to make good decisions, then efficiency becomes the by-product. You may wonder how that will make them more efficient. It does simply because it is part of what they are doing rather than stopping and looking for an answer from you at the most inopportune time; the most inopportune time for them, you, and most importantly the customer.

My challenge for you from this chapter is, go back and look at your workload, determine if you are the best one for that task,

"Confidence is paramount to making your team less dependent on you."

or if you can train someone to do it. This, in turn, will give them a better understanding of what must happen to run the business effectively, and better sets them up for further development. It also assures them that you have confidence in their ability to do more than they are currently doing and preparing them for their next role within the organization. Afterall, we should always be training our replacement. Effective leadership involves balancing your own workload while empowering and developing your team members. By relinquishing unnecessary tasks and guiding your team, you can foster a culture of growth, independence, and efficiency.

Reflecting on "Busy vs. Effective"

1. How often do you find yourself busy with tasks that could be delegated to your team members? Reflect on the impact of constantly taking on tasks that could be opportunities for growth and development within your team. Consider how empowering your team and delegating effectively can lead to increased productivity and personal growth.

_____

_____

_____

_____

2. In what ways have you unintentionally created dependency within your team? Reflect on instances where team members rely heavily on your involvement and decision-making, rather than feeling empowered to take the initiative. Consider the importance of fostering a culture of independence and confidence among your team members.

_____

_____

_____

_____

3. Are you investing enough time in developing your team members' skills and abilities? Reflect on the value of training and mentoring your team to perform tasks that align with their roles and future aspirations. Consider how this investment in their growth can enhance overall efficiency and create a more resilient and capable team.

_____

_____

_____

Notes

Chapter 4

Counseling vs. Coaching

Leadership encompasses more than simply guiding teams; it entails nurturing the growth and development of individual team members. Two powerful approaches that aid in this process are coaching and counseling. Coaching is a proactive and empowering process that unlocks untapped potential by providing guidance, feedback, and support. It aims to enhance skills, foster self-awareness, and cultivate high performance. On the other hand, counseling delves into deeper emotions, offering a space for reflection, empathy, and guidance during personal or professional difficulties. It focuses on providing solace and overcoming obstacles that hinder progress.

To unlock the full potential of our teams and individual members, it is crucial to discern when to employ each approach. By doing so, leaders gain considerable influence in propelling their teams towards excellence and fostering a culture of growth, resilience, and shared success. In this chapter, we will explore the transformative realms of coaching and counseling, where leaders rise to new heights by empowering their teams and nurturing personal and professional well-being.

Coaching and counseling play distinct roles in the development of individuals. While counseling may seem like a means of redirecting individuals after they make mistakes, coaching takes a proactive approach by making them better. Coaching creates an atmosphere that encourages transparency, allowing individuals to seek guidance and advice. Most individuals are aware of their mistakes and, when given the opportunity, they want to improve and achieve better results. Reflecting on our own experiences, we can recall moments when we made mistakes and hoped our superiors would not find out.

Being reactive achieves little, whereas proper planning lays the foundation for success. Unfortunately, we often spend significantly more time counseling our teams on aspects that did not go as expected. We focus on areas where they fall short, such as sales performance, customer care, or communication skills. Consequently, they become less likely to approach us, fearing another counseling session. This pattern hampers their growth and our ability to coach effectively.

We all know not much happens when we are being reactive. We should also know, with proper planning, we are laying the foundation for success. All too often when it comes to our teams, the time we spend with them is spent counseling them on something that did not go the way we thought it should. When this happens, they typically start to withdraw from communicating effectively with their customers and colleagues. Quite frankly, they are not communicating with you either, or at least the way you want them to. Often, the reason they are not communicating with you the way you want them to or asking the questions that you want them to ask is because you are always counseling them. We usually only catch them doing the things they could have done more effectively. You find you are continually asking yourself why

"Being reactive achieves little, whereas proper planning lays the foundation for success."

this person is not getting it. The reason they are not getting it is because you are doing just that, you are catching them doing things that they may not be good at yet, or they may not yet understand how to accomplish the task to deliver the desired results. We think that if we step on their toes when they do not meet our expectations that they will miraculously improve.

Unfortunately, we usually spend too much time counseling and not enough time coaching our teams. I will assure you, if you coach more, you will counsel less. Let me give you a few examples. When someone is not meeting your expectations, we should clearly state where they are falling short, then we can take the opportunity to give the needed guidance taking them in the desired direction. Now we are not just telling them what they are doing wrong and that we expect more from them, but we are showing them how to get the results that we are looking for them to deliver.

In my experience of leading teams, I have found that leadership is extremely similar to parenting. As parents, we are always encouraging our kids to get better at something, try something new, or explaining why things happen the way they do. For example, what if we reprimanded our kids every time they fell while learning to walk, or we got mad at them when they skinned their knees while learning to ride a bike. Instead, we pick them up, make sure they will be ok, and encourage them to try it again, and again until they get up and walk or ride their bike without training wheels. Even after they learn to walk and ride their bike, they will still make mistakes causing them to fall or crash. In these instances, we still encourage them to keep after it, so they can continue to improve. As a result of us encouraging our kids to continue to improve, they start to take the initiative to try things on their own. Perhaps, this is where innovation truly starts.

"Unfortunately, we usually spend too much time counseling and not enough time coaching our teams."

If leading is similar to parenting, because as parents we are coaching our kids to improve, then we need to harness every opportunity to encourage our team members to get better. Coaching is initiative-taking, counseling is reacting. So, if we are only counseling them, that means we are only catching them doing the things we wish they would do differently. This makes them less likely to seek you out when they are struggling with something, because they are not looking for that next counseling session.

Let's look at this from a coaching standpoint, when we coach them through obstacles, they become more confident with what they are doing. Perhaps, more importantly you become more approachable. Let's elaborate on that a little bit more. If you are talking to them about how they can get better, they will want to have a two-sided conversation with you. More times than not, when we start with counseling, they usually just mentally shut down until they get out of our office. Nobody wins in these situations. We need to have regular coaching sessions rather than counseling sessions when something is wrong.

When we spend more time coaching, they come seeking your help before they make a mistake. They are there asking for help during the situation, rather than reacting to it afterwards. To shift this dynamic, we should spend more time coaching and less time counseling. When someone falls short of expectations, it is essential to provide constructive feedback and demonstrate how to improve. Coaching involves showing individuals the path to desired outcomes rather than solely pointing out their mistakes. Initiating coaching sessions instead of counseling sessions creates an environment where individuals feel supported and confident. They become more likely to seek guidance before making mistakes and approach us during challenging situations.

Making an intentional effort to counsel less and coach more is vital. Both counseling and coaching have their place, but knowing when to employ each approach is paramount. In moments that necessitate counseling, ask yourself whether you have adequately demonstrated the desired behavior. If not, there is a greater opportunity for coaching. By actively embracing the role of a coach, we fulfill the needs of our teams. This approach fosters open-mindedness, empowering team members to coach each other and face challenges collectively.

As we prioritize coaching over counseling, the desired results compound. We become approachable leaders who inspire their team members to bring their innovative ideas for guidance and support. This collective intelligence allows us to challenge the status quo and become industry leaders. By actively engaging in coaching and counseling with intention and balance, we unlock the full potential of our teams and foster an environment of continuous growth and excellence. Remember, coaching fosters growth, builds confidence, and encourages initiative-taking problem-solving within your team. By shifting your primary focus from counseling to coaching, you can empower your team members to learn, improve, and become more self-sufficient in their roles.

Reflecting on "Counseling vs. Coaching"

1. Reflect on your current leadership approach: Do you find yourself counseling your team members more often than coaching them? Consider the impact of counseling versus coaching on their growth, confidence, and overall performance. How can you shift your focus to become a more effective coach and guide for your team?

_____

_____

_____

2. Think about a recent situation where you had to address a team member's performance issue. Did you approach it from a counseling or coaching perspective? What were the outcomes of your approach? Consider how coaching, by providing guidance and showing them how to improve, can create a more collaborative and growth-oriented atmosphere.

_____

_____

_____

3. Consider your accessibility and approachability as a leader: Are your team members comfortable seeking your guidance and support before they encounter challenges, or do they avoid approaching you until after they have made a mistake? Reflect on how you can create an environment that encourages open communication and proactive coaching, allowing your team members to seek guidance and share ideas more readily.

_____

_____

_____

Notes

Chapter 5

Perception vs. Reality

In the realm of leadership, where challenges and uncertainties are abundant, our perception and the true reality often dance an intricate tango. Perception, simply put, is how we see and interpret the world around us, influenced by our thoughts, beliefs, and emotions. It acts as a filter, coloring our understanding and shaping our actions. Reality, on the other hand, is the unvarnished truth, the undeniable facts and circumstances that exist, independent of our perceptions. By unraveling the delicate balance between how we perceive things and the truths that underpin them, we uncover the potential to transform adversity into opportunity, cultivate resilience, and inspire others through unwavering optimism.

In this ever-changing and often challenging world, it is easy to become consumed by the negative aspects and setbacks that arise or are waiting to arise around the corner. However, great leaders understand the power of positivity and how it can have a transformative effect on you and your team both personally and professionally. By consciously seeking out the positive aspect in every situation, catching people doing things right, and promoting them to do it again, you can create a culture that fosters growth, self-motivation, and unrivaled success for all involved. In this chapter, we will explore the art of recognizing and amplifying positivity, enabling you as the leader to unlock your team's full potential and in most cases set the stage for ongoing personal and professional development. People will always do more of what gets recognized and praised.

It takes true intentionality to see the positive in every situation. Every day we will run into situations or obstacles that could be construed as bad or less than desirable. Naturally, we as humans are hardwired to see the negative first as a defensive instinct. Finding the positive aspect in every situation does not come naturally, this is a learned behavior, and it is something you must practice ongoingly to really be effective at it.

Let me give you an example. Are you someone that gets furious when someone cuts you off in traffic? If so, you have the opportunity to find the positive in this situation so you can make these situations better. Now, I am not saying that you should be happy with someone cutting you off in traffic, what I am saying is there is still a positive aspect looming, waiting to be identified.

It is easy to allow a bad moment in our day, get in our head, then give it subliminal permission to ruin the rest of our day. Truly what happened is we had a bad moment and we chose to let it control us. When we do this, we tell ourselves it is going to be one of those days. Then when someone encounters you and asks you how your day is going, you shrug them off, or you express to them how badly your day has gone thus far. We all know misery loves company. Then they proceed to tell you something that went bad or wrong for them as well. Who do you think wins in these situations? Absolutely no one on either side wins, because we justify the negative mindset, and condemn the rest of the day to fester and spread to the rest of

"People will always do more
of what gets recognized
and praised."

the team. At least, this is the perception we have created in our minds.

Let's break that down a little more. Life is not made-up by how someone drives around you in traffic. The things that are important to you are the things that fuel your "Y" (remember your Y is your purpose). So, if your "Y" is your family, then you must ask yourself is everyone in my family, ok? Hopefully that answer is yes, and if it is, now is the moment to be thankful that the vehicle only cut you off and did not cause a terribly tragic accident. So, what I am saying is we must put things into perspective.

When we put things in perspective it allows us to see what is truly happening. Let's go back to the car that cut you off earlier. You had to slow down a bit, quite frankly you were probably speeding, and now that you slowed down, you probably won't take that chance to run through that yellow light as you try to scurry through to get to where you're going 45 seconds sooner. Now, while you are waiting at that light you see there is an officer sitting right there in the other direction waiting for his light to turn green, all while watching to see who, if anyone, runs the light at which you are now waiting.

So, in this scenario, I have explained two perspectives. There is one perspective asking yourself what is important to you, and one is putting yourself back into check so you can keep things in order. More times than not when you watch that light turn red right in front of you, you say to yourself, "if that guy had not cut me off, I could have made that light", then you spit out a few choice words that only you can hear. Now ask yourself, *Did this really help the situation*? You do not need to answer that because we both know the answer.

These scenarios happen to our team members every single day

and it is our responsibility to help them see the bigger picture, but we cannot help them see the bigger picture if we are stuck in the same routine. It is up to us to find the unseen benefit in every situation, whether it is for ourselves or for the people around us. When we help someone find the positive aspect in a certain situation, we, in turn, help them put their day back in order. Because when we have negative thoughts, those thoughts promote more negative thoughts. Then when we encounter other people, we spread our negativity onto them, and they start having negative thoughts and looking for things that are not going right for them as well, so that they can spend time together with you in the self-pity party that you both are now having.

However, when we help them find the positive aspects, we are helping them to push their reset button and we are giving them an opportunity to have a fresh start for the day. This allows them to have their bad moment or possibly a few moments without turning those moments into a dreadful day that bleeds over into the rest of our team and everyone else that they may encounter. When this happens and the negativity spreads throughout, the next thing you know is your team is telling you it has been one of those days. They are telling themselves they cannot make anyone happy today, or everyone that has come in thus far today has had a chip on their shoulder.

Newsflash, people do not show up expecting you to make them angry. We let things get in our way and control our day which in turn, shows in our actions and emotions in front of our customers setting the tone for them to be defensive.

Now we have the situation of nothing going right. Let us reset that moment of the day, or help someone reset their day, to prevent it from continuing to fester. Now you arrive at work, everyone is safe, you start going around to check the

"However, when we help them find the positive aspects, we are helping them to push their reset button and we are giving them an opportunity to have a fresh start for the day."

emotional state and well-being of your team now that we are not wallowing in our own self-pity. We have time to connect with our team, we have time to help them through whatever obstacle they may have run into this morning, we help them put things into perspective, and help them push their reset button so they can set the stage to have an enjoyable and productive day.

When they are having an enjoyable and productive day, your customers will enjoy the time they have with them as well. So, it is ultra important for us to find the unseen benefit in every situation and be that bright spot for our team members daily. It just may be the only bright spot they get to start their day.

It is our responsibility as leaders to get our teams to look at what could go right, rather than what could go wrong. This does not happen if you, as their leader, are wallowing in your own self-pity or moping in your office hoping today is going to be better than yesterday. It is our responsibility to go out and make today better than yesterday for everyone involved. So, your *Mile One* today, tomorrow and every day afterwards is to go out and set the tone for your team in a positive way. Go be the bright spot that they are desperately needing.

Remember, a key element of leadership is creating an environment where positivity thrives. By finding and pointing out the positive aspect in every situation, catching people doing something right, and promoting them to do it again, leaders inspire their team to exceed expectations and promote them in ways in which they believe they can achieve greatness. Embrace the power of positivity and watch as your workplace transforms into a hub of growth, innovation, and unwavering motivation.

Great leaders do not create followers; they create the atmosphere to create more leaders. Additionally, as a leader,

"Great leaders do not create followers; they create the atmosphere to create more leaders."

your mindset and attitude significantly influence the overall morale and performance of your team. By intentionally seeking out the positive, highlighting strengths, and fostering a culture of optimism, you can unlock the full potential of your team members and create an environment that fuels ongoing personal and professional development. Now, go create some additional leaders so they can amplify the elements of this chapter.

Reflecting on "Perception vs. Reality"

1. Reflect on your typical response to challenging situations. Do you find yourself naturally focusing on the negative aspects or setbacks? How does this mindset affect your overall well-being and the way you lead your team? Consider the potential benefits of consciously seeking out the positive aspects in every situation and how it can contribute to a more productive and optimistic work environment.

_____

_____

_____

_____

2. Think about a recent instance where you encountered a setback or obstacle. Did you immediately identify any positive aspects or hidden benefits in that situation? How did your mindset and approach impact the outcome and the way you communicated with your team? Reflect on how you can cultivate the habit of recognizing the unseen benefits and helping others do the same, fostering a more resilient and solution-oriented team culture.

_____

_____

_____

_____

3. Assess your role as a leader in promoting positivity within your team. Are you actively catching and acknowledging your team members' positive contributions? How does recognizing and amplifying positivity impact their motivation, engagement, and personal growth? Consider specific strategies you can implement to create a culture where positivity is celebrated, and individuals are empowered to

embrace their potential as leaders.

_____

_____

_____

_____

Notes

Chapter 6

Motivation vs. Inspiration

In the world of leadership, the ability to inspire and motivate others lies at the heart of creating lasting impact and driving extraordinary results. While motivation and inspiration may seem like interchangeable concepts, they possess distinct qualities that shape our approach to leading and influencing others. Motivation is a powerful force that propels individuals forward, fueled by external factors such as rewards, incentives, or short-term goals. It ignites a spark, urging action in pursuit of specific objectives.

On the other hand, inspiration transcends the temporary bursts of motivation. It taps into the deeper aspirations, values, and purposes that reside within individuals, stirring their hearts and minds to envision and strive for something greater. In this chapter, we embark on the exploration of the dynamic interplay between inspiration and motivation, understanding their unique roles and the transformative impact they hold. By harnessing both the power to inspire and the art of motivation, leaders unlock the potential to create a shared vision that transcends personal aspirations, igniting a collective drive towards excellence, innovation, and meaningful achievements. Let's dive into the realms of

"By harnessing both the power to inspire and the art of motivation, leaders unlock the potential to create a shared vision that transcends personal aspirations, igniting a collective drive towards excellence, innovation, and meaningful achievements."

inspiration and motivation, where leaders rise to new heights by nurturing the spirit, fueling passion, and empowering individuals to embark on a purpose-driven journey towards shared success.

Inspiring your team to give their best at work is a crucial aspect of effective leadership. From my experience, without inspiration, we must continuously motivate our team to just do the basics of the job we hired them to do.

However, when we inspire them with the vision of what we want to accomplish as an organization, and what the desired goal entails, that now becomes the mission at hand. That is when our team members take charge and become engaged, which leads to them bringing new initiatives, a sense of ownership, and belief from within that it can and will be accomplished. They start to visualize in their mind accomplishing whatever the mission may be. This is when we get everyone rowing in the same direction and preventing or eliminating the friction points.

I want to explain the difference between inspiring your team to get the best results and continually trying to motivate them. I hope by this point in the book that you have learned that effective leadership is about creating an environment in which your team can thrive, achieve their goals, and reach their full potential. One of the fundamental aspects of effective leadership is inspiring and motivating your team to perform at their best. However, there is a significant difference between inspiring and motivating your team, and understanding this difference is crucial to achieve outstanding results.

Motivating your team can be effective, but it is usually short lived. Motivation is an external force that drives behavior. When you motivate your team, you provide incentives, rewards, or consequences that you hope encourages them to perform. Motivation involves setting goals, providing feedback, and holding people accountable for their performance. Motivation can be useful to accomplish a one-time or rare task, but if overused or misapplied, it will usually have negative effects. When people feel forced to perform, they will become resentful, stressed, and disengaged, which can ultimately harm productivity, efficiency, and team morale. This usually leads to an unwelcome environment that leads to turnover.

As I write this chapter, I reflect on a particular meeting I have held many times and continue to hold depending on the audience and situation at hand. I have found through my experience that these meetings have been and still are very effective with my teams and individual team members.

As our team members feel the pressure of a heavy workload, they usually start to drift into the mindset of that they cannot perform because of whatever they are or have been struggling with. So, in those meetings I have each of them write down three things that they feel like they cannot accomplish. Taking those same three things, I asked them to shift their mind to *I can because*, instead of *I cannot because*. Removing the "not" from the same phrase, they usually start to see how it can be accomplished, instead of focusing on what they feel is an impossible obstacle.

Let me help you visualize one of these meetings. As we get started, I usually give everyone an index card with "I can't because" written on the card. "I can't" is written on the first line with the "'T" near the far right of the card, "because" is written on the second line, with three additional lines below. I ask them to write down the three things they can't do because of whatever the circumstances may be. Then I ask them to tell me why they can't do it. After they elaborate for a few minutes, I ask them to take a pair of scissors and cut the "'T'" from the index card. The card now reads "I can because," then I give them an example of how they can do one of the things they have written down. I also ask them to now tell me what they can do, rather than what they can't do with the other items listed. The intent here is to shift them into thinking about what they can do, instead of telling me why they cannot do something.

It is common for us as humans to withdraw a bit when we run into a struggle. The true intent of these meetings is to help bring the power and collaboration of the team back into focus. As each team member starts looking at it from *I can because*, you can usually feel the power sway, to what is sometimes quite magical. The chatter in the room becomes more encouraging as they start to share their obstacles with each other. As they share with each other, they also start sharing ideas of what they can do to overcome their obstacles. Progress happens when we shift our minds from the situation being an obstacle to an opportunity. Their obstacle becomes the opportunity when they see and understand what they can do about it. This is when the power of inspiration starts to arise.

We will talk about creating impactful memories in a later chapter. Until then, I cannot help but reflect on holding one of these meetings several years ago. As Crystal, a longtime employee of mine, who still works for me today. She told me years later that one particular meeting was life-changing for her, both personally and professionally. The week prior to that meeting she sat in my office, tears streaming down her face, telling me that her job was not fun anymore. She later told me that cutting the "'t'" from that note card reprogrammed her brain to think differently, think positively. She realized she could do something to make any situation better, even if it did not completely solve the situation. In her mind, this shift in thinking changed everything. She constantly told herself what she could do, focusing on the impacts she could make and having that mindset unleashed a new level of confidence! Crystal has grown significantly since then, and now has a team of her own. I smile every time I hear one of her team members object with an obstacle, and without skipping a beat she says, "Tell them what you can do, not what you can't do." If you asked her today to produce that cut up note card, I have no doubt that she could produce it rather quickly.

It is common for us to build roadblocks in our minds as we run into obstacles or pressures that arise from certain situations. However, by helping and encouraging them to look at it from a unique perspective they started to assure themselves that they could and would be able to overcome almost any obstacle. This simple exercise helps build their own confidence, which in turn inspires them to overcome the pressure on their own by looking at what they can do, and what they can control.

It is important to recognize that motivation alone is not enough to create ongoing, high-performing teams. All of this must be combined with inspiration to create a culture of excellence and continuous improvement.

Inspiration comes from within, and it is about tapping into the passions and aspirations of each of your team members. When you inspire your team, you ignite their creativity, energy, and commitment, and they become motivated to work towards a shared vision. Inspiration involves leading by example, setting lofty standards, and creating a culture of trust, respect, and collaboration.

Inspiring your team also involves creating a compelling vision that resonates with their aspirations and values. It means communicating this vision in a clear, concise, and memorable

"Tell them what you can do,
not what you can't do."

way. When you inspire your team, you provide them with a sense of purpose and direction, and they become motivated to achieve their goals and contribute to the success of the team.

Additionally, inspiring your team involves creating a sense of purpose and meaning that motivates them to perform at their best. As you can see, inspiring your team to give their best at work requires a combination of leadership skills, clear communication, and a positive, trusting, and collaborative culture. By demonstrating your own enthusiasm, providing clear direction and support, and recognizing your team's successes, you can help to create a team that is inspired, engaged, and committed to achieving and exceeding their personal goals, and the goals of the organization.

Effective leadership involves both inspiring and motivating your team. Inspiration ignites passion and creativity, taps into intrinsic motivation, and creates a culture of trust and respect. Motivation drives behavior and provides incentives to achieve short-term goals. By understanding the difference between the two and using them appropriately, you can create high-performing teams that achieve extraordinary results while fostering a fulfilling, inviting, and rewarding work environment.

Reflecting on "Motivation vs. Inspiration"

1. Reflect on a time when you felt inspired by a leader or a vision. How did that inspiration impact your motivation and performance? How can you incorporate elements of inspiration into your own leadership style?

_____

_____

_____

_____

2. Consider the exercise mentioned in the chapter, where team members shifted their mindset from _I can't do this_ to _I can do this._ How can you apply this approach to help your team overcome obstacles and build their confidence? What other techniques can you use to encourage a positive and initiative-taking mindset within your team?

_____

_____

_____

_____

3. Reflect on your own leadership style. Do you tend to rely more on motivation or inspiration? How can you strike a balance between the two to create a culture of excellence and continuous improvement within your team?

_____

_____

_____

_____

Notes

Chapter 7

Trust

Trust is a fundamental aspect of Leadership. It is essential for building lasting relationships with your team members. Without trust, do we really have anything? Think about that for a few moments. Trust is the foundation to bringing all the content of the previous and following chapters together. Strong levels of trust can and will help us build meaningful relationships in our personal and professional lives.

Trust is essential for effective Leadership; it creates the platform for collaboration. With trust you can challenge the status quo because your team trusts that you will not lead them down the wrong path. If we, as a team, are trying something new, and it is not going as expected, they trust that you will create the redirection that is needed at the time. It also creates a platform for your team to feel heard when they produce ideas to make changes or to go in a different direction.

Trust can and will help us build meaningful relationships in our personal and professional lives. Trust does not happen overnight. It does not happen at first sight. It happens because of ongoing consistent trustworthy actions and behaviors your team sees in you, and that you see in them. In this chapter we will go over the power of trust, and I will give you an example and actions needed to build and maintain elevated levels of trust.

We must be effective communicators to build layers of trust. After all, how can we build trust if we rarely or never communicate with the ones around us? Better yet, how can we build trust if our communication is one-sided? We must be intentional with all our communication with our team members, and it must be a two-way street. A key element of communicating is always being transparent with our teams. If you are not transparent with them, they will feel like you are always hiding something, or you have a different agenda than what you are expressing to them.

We must be able to openly admit our mistakes. Don't just stop at admitting the mistake, but also, when appropriate, genuinely asking for their help with correcting the mistake. Ask how it could have been done differently. Afterall, we do not have to have all the answers. As a team, we are building the foundation to use all the collective brain power of the team.

As leaders we should respect our team's personal and professional boundaries and allow them to process the situation without micromanaging every aspect of their input and work. Micromanagement is one of the fastest ways to erode and destroy the trust you have spent so much time building. If there is only one thing you take away from this book, always remember that micromanagement is toxic on all levels, and your team will run from it.

Another key element of trust is following through on your commitments. They look at us for our support, so when we make a commitment to them to do something regardless of

"Micromanagement is one of the fastest ways to erode and destroy the trust you have spent so much time building."

how big or small, we must follow through on it, or at least circle back to them to let them know why you could not follow through with whatever it was.

Remember, you can have all the best intentions, but if you do not follow through on them, your team will see this as a lack of care. And to make it worse, they sometimes even see it as a lack of care for them as your team member. So, it is worth saying again, follow through on your commitments.

Another extremely essential element of building trust is truly listening to your team members. Everyone wants to be heard. When you are talking with one of your team members, put your phone down, and give them your undivided attention so you can actively listen. You may be surprised at what you can learn about them both personally and professionally.

Listen intently. One of the elements of a good listener is the ability to demonstrate empathy. Most of the time when our team members have asked to have a few minutes with us, they have put themselves in a vulnerable position. When they become vulnerable with you, no matter the situation, they are saying, usually without saying, they trust you, or they really need to trust you in this situation.

Lead by example. There are key elements that need to be displayed and actions that need to be taken to build a foundation to foster trust. You must walk the walk, not just talk the talk. Our team members pay attention to everything we do. Remember you are always setting the example. Do not ever use phrases like, "Because I am the boss," or "I can because of who I am." Your aspiring team members will be emulating you because they want to continue to grow and be like you as well. Make sure you are acting in a way you want emulated in both your personal and professional life 24 hours a day, 7 days a week, 365 days a year. How you do one thing

"How you do one thing is how you do everything."

is how you do everything.

As for setting the example, this may be one of the toughest ones for me to give a good example, as trust is a feeling very much like love. Love is tough to explain through words because it is more of a feeling that grows or fades over time, and it is influenced by our actions and behaviors. The same thing is true with trust, it either grows or erodes over time and it too is driven by our actions and behaviors. I will try to give you an example of the true power of trust in leadership, and its impact on every aspect of any business or organization.

We live in a world where mergers or acquisitions are the norm. One of the first concerns that comes up is, "Will I get to keep my job, or will I be laid off?" Imagine a newly acquired company led by a proven leader who is determined to make an impact within their industry. In their quest for success, they assemble a team of individuals with diverse skills and backgrounds. Most of these individuals were already on this team prior to the acquisition of the company, but not necessarily in the right position. With realignment that compliments each team member's strengths with the right position, they now are starting to feel like they are part of a team rather than just working a job. Then comes the true turning point when the leader establishes a culture of trust within the organization. They then openly share their vision, goals, and challenges with the team, demonstrating vulnerability and transparency.

In turn, the team reciprocates by offering their full commitment, dedication, and unwavering support. Each team member trusts that their colleagues will deliver on their responsibilities and collaborate effectively. This trust allows them to work together seamlessly, leveraging each other's strengths and expertise. They openly communicate, share ideas, and engage in healthy debates, confident that their opinions are valued and respected. As a result, the newly acquired company experiences remarkable growth that fosters innovation and is achieving milestones that seemed impossible just a few months previous.

Trust is a critical aspect of leadership of any type. It requires endless effort and attention. Trust is the foundation for building productive teams that deliver results. It is the component that allows you to continue to cultivate the desired culture. It is the component that sets the stage for employee retention.

Remember, trust is extremely fragile, and can be lost in a flash. Do not be afraid to apologize when needed. With that said, if you follow the elements listed in this chapter, and always lead by example, even when you are not in the presence of your team, you will be continuing to build layers of trust. With those layers of trust, your team will do anything, go through anything, and try anything right there next to you. That is when you start to create a dynasty that will be desired and respected by many.

Reflecting on "Trust"

1. Why is trust considered a fundamental aspect of leadership? How does it impact relationships with team members?

_____

_____

_____

_____

2. Reflect on a time when you made a mistake as a leader. How did you manage it? Did you openly admit the mistake and ask for help in correcting it? How did this impact the trust within your team?

_____

_____

_____

_____

3. Consider the importance of active listening in building trust. How can you improve your listening skills to create an environment where team members feel heard and valued?

_____

_____

_____

_____

Bonus question.
Reflect on a time when someone in a leadership position failed to follow through on their commitments. How did it affect your perception of them and the trust you had in their leadership? What can you do as a leader to ensure you follow through on your commitments?

Notes

Chapter 8

Collaboration

None of us will ever have all the answers. With that said, we will always be stronger when we come together to work towards a common goal. In this chapter we will explore the power that is created when we bring all our team members together to create a collaborative unit. Doing this sets the stage for all departments to work together, in turn, helping to remove the silo mentality.

To be an effective leader you will need to create and encourage the collaboration of the entire team. Then with the collaboration of your team pulling together to maximize their individual strengths, the answers, direction, and execution will often be at its peak. Setting the stage for collaboration lets your team know that you trust them and empower them to keep things in motion. I will break down some of the key elements to creating the platform for collaboration of the entire team.

We must first emphasize the importance of collaboration. As a leader, you must constantly build on the values of collaboration and teamwork. Encourage your team to work together, share ideas, and support each other. Make it clear

"Setting the stage for collaboration lets your team know that you trust them and empower them to keep things in motion."

that you value collaboration and that it is an essential component of achieving ongoing success and growth.

You cannot have collaboration without a prominent level of trust. We must cultivate and continue to cultivate a culture of trust within your team by being open and transparent, communicating clearly and consistently, and always leading by example. When team members trust each other, they are more likely to work together effectively and achieve better results by focusing on their strengths while supporting the vision.

Every team member has their own strengths and skills. As a leader, it is important to recognize and leverage these strengths to achieve the best possible results. Encourage team members to share their expertise and help each other to develop new skills, and become more efficient as a team.

Another necessary element for effective collaboration requires open communication and dialogue. Encourage your team to communicate openly and honestly with each other and make it clear that feedback is essential for improvement for personal, professional, and organizational growth.

We talked about being visible in an earlier chapter. As we are out and about catching people working, we will have the opportunity to create impromptu conversations. Let's call these conversations drive-bys. Regular drive-bys and team meetings are necessary and will help to ensure that everyone is on the same page, all while identifying additional opportunities for efficiency and growth. But drive-bys, and team meetings alone are not enough to encourage effective collaboration.

Regularly scheduled meetings are vital for effective leadership and collaboration within teams and the entire organization.

These meetings serve as a platform for open communication, goal setting, problem-solving, and fostering a sense of unity among all team members. By creating regularly scheduled meetings, leaders can ensure that everyone is on the same page and working towards common goals and objectives.

Leaders can utilize these gatherings to set clear expectations, provide guidance, encourage collaboration, and offer support to team members. With open and transparent communication, leaders can address any concerns or challenges faced by the team and provide needed feedback. Additionally, meetings provide a chance for leaders to recognize and highlight the accomplishments or bright spots of the team or team members. This helps boost morale and offers inspiration to repeat the action or accomplishment.

Regular meetings also play a crucial role in fostering collaboration among team members. By bringing everyone together, these gatherings facilitate the exchange of ideas, sharing of knowledge, and cross-department cooperation. Collaborative discussions during meetings encourage diverse perspectives, leading to innovative solutions, improved decision-making, and team buy-in. These interactions allow team members to learn from one another, build relationships, and establish trust, which enhances overall teamwork and productivity.

Going beyond team meetings and drive-bys, organization-wide meetings are essential for aligning all departmental teams towards common goals. Regularly scheduled company-wide gatherings help with the spread of vital information, such as organizational updates, strategic initiatives, and changes in policies or procedures. This ensures that almost every employee is aware of the broader context and direction of the organization, enabling them to align their work accordingly. Such alignment is critical for creating a unified and coordinated effort, minimizing, or hopefully eliminating silos, and maximizing the overall effectiveness of the organization.

Regularly scheduled meetings throughout the organization are a fundamental element of effective leadership and collaboration within the organization. These meetings provide leaders with a platform to communicate expectations, offer support, and recognize achievements. They also foster collaboration among team members, encouraging the exchange of ideas, knowledge sharing, and cross-departmental cooperation. Organization-wide meetings ensure that everyone is aligned with the organization's vision, goals, and initiatives. By prioritizing and investing in regular meetings, organizations can enhance collaboration, drive innovation, and achieve their objectives more effectively and efficiently.

Additionally, creating diversity of varying thoughts and experiences throughout our organizations can be powerful for our teams to support each other. As a leader we must encourage diversity and inclusion within our teams, and ensure that everyone feels valued, heard, and respected for their individual and team contributions.

I want to give you an example of using diversity of varying thoughts to promote collaboration and to challenge the status quo. When a certain situation arises that requires a process change, or if the organization is developing something new and innovative, or just simply trying to problem solve, it is not usually healthy and certainly not the most productive for you as the leader to always have all the answers.

I have found through my experience that when we need to change something or develop something new, that bringing someone from each team or department helps us look at the

"As a leader we must encourage diversity and inclusion within our teams, and ensure that everyone feels valued, heard, and respected for their individual and team contributions."

situation in varying ways. We assemble a willing team, which consists of 4-7 delegates from varying teams or departments. We then explain the desired outcome, and or the vision of something new. We are starting with the end in mind.

Then, on the whiteboard, we start drawing things out using the input from all the newly assembled team members. Some of these members work in the areas of the change and some work in other areas. This creates the platform for us to have input from the functional side (the ones performing the task or process), and from what could be the customer or end-user side. We draw out a new process or path and challenge each other to think about possible obstacles, and challenges. At the conclusion of the meeting or meetings, we have a process or direction that our team members created within your presence, ensuring buy-in.

This naturally generates buy-in because it is their thoughts and ideas. Sometimes you will need to bring the team back together to verify or modify elements that may need to be changed as added information arises from putting it into action. This is an internal process improvement team or focus group that promotes collaboration and inclusion, making each team member feel valued. This type of meeting promotes the development of each team member as they start to see and understand the inner workings of each department, giving them a better understanding of how it all comes together.

Always celebrate successes together as a team. Celebrating the successes, and the acknowledgement of their contributions to the team is essential with each team member. It will also show them that you are taking notice of what they bring to the collective team. Celebrating successes can also help to build morale, boost motivation, and reinforce the value of collaboration.

As we all know, conflicts are inevitable with any team. As they arise, we must address them as early and proactively as possible. You, as the leader, must also address them privately and constructively, as there is always something to learn from every situation that arises. You must continuously encourage our team members to address conflicts respectfully and directly with each other while keeping the team-first mindset, and you must provide guidance and support as needed.

Overall, effective collaboration requires a strong culture of trust, open communication, and a willingness to leverage individual strengths. By emphasizing the value of collaboration, fostering open dialogue, holding regularly scheduled meetings, and celebrating successes and bright spots, you can build a strong, motivated team that achieves extraordinary results.

Reflecting on "Collaboration"

1. Reflect on the strengths and skills of each team member. How can you recognize and leverage these strengths to enhance collaboration and achieve better results? What strategies can you implement to encourage knowledge-sharing, skill development, and mutual support among team members?

_____

_____

_____

2. Reflect on the importance of regularly scheduled meetings in promoting collaboration. How can you optimize team meetings to foster collaboration, goal setting, problem-solving, and a sense of unity? What specific techniques or approaches can you employ to ensure that meetings are productive and meaningful for the team?

_____

_____

_____

3. Consider the overall message of the chapter: collaboration is a powerful force that enhances teamwork and achieves industry-leading results. How can you apply the principles and strategies discussed in this chapter to foster a collaborative culture within your team or organization? What specific actions can you take to promote collaboration and maximize the potential of your team?

_____

_____

_____

Notes

Chapter 9
Memories

Life is made up of a plethora of memories, most of them being a moment in time that was impactful for some reason or another. Take a moment to reflect. Reminisce over the things that mean the most to you, or that you may have witnessed. Most all of them took about a minute. Some might have taken longer to come together, but your memory of it only lasts about a minute.

We affect people's lives every single day. Are you affecting their lives in a way that will leave a lasting memory? It warms my heart when I encounter someone that I have not seen for weeks, months, or even years, and after we greet each other and check on each other's families, it is common for them to say, "You know, do you remember this?" They speak of something that happened to them in or around my presence that changed their life forever. I am forever grateful for those conversations. Those are absolutely some of the best words that you can hear when you are talking with someone whether you are talking with them every day, once a week, once a year or just the occasional contact passing through somewhere.

"We affect people's lives every single day. Are you affecting their lives in a way that will leave a lasting memory?"

When you really connect with someone, you learn what makes them tick, you learn why they do what they do. This is their "Y," their Y is their purpose to do what they do. When you learn what their Y is, it makes it easier to make connections that create those memories. Without the intentionality of learning about them, truly what is important to them, this opportunity is often missed. One of the most important things for us to do is connect with our team, and I mean truly connect with them. It is about making those connections and helping our teams reach their goals and aspirations.

You see in business we think that when we give someone a job, that job becomes their purpose. The reality is the job only becomes their enabler to their purpose. If we find out what their purpose entails, then we can mold their job around ways for them to enhance, work on, or have time for their true purpose.

I will give you an example. It is all too often that we have an employee come to us in the midafternoon and says, "Boss I think I ate something bad for lunch. I have not been able to stay out of the bathroom since we got back. I went with Johnny, Bill, and Mike, and they all seem to be ok." What that person is afraid to tell you is that their child has a game that evening, and they are not going to miss it. But he is struggling with telling you the truth. The reality is you should already know that they have a game that evening.

You should be out there asking how prepared they are for the game and what they think their chances are of winning. You should also create the atmosphere and safe space for them to be able to check out long before game time. Then you go out and ask them about the game the next morning.

In these types of scenarios, one of the worst possible things you can ask them is, "What did you do last night?" If you ask those questions, they automatically know that you really did not pay attention to what they have going on in their own lives. So do not ask what they did last night, instead you ask, "How did the game go?" Better yet, send them a text during the game, stating I am checking on you. That lets them know that you are truly connected and care about what is important to them.

I just gave one example, but there are hundreds. I will give you one more. As we passed through our offices, warehouses, production facilities and we asked people how they were doing, or what they were planning to do that weekend, or what did they do over the past weekend. They give us so much information when we do this.

They tell us, "It was my anniversary," or "It was my daughter's birthday," or "It was my wife's birthday." "We are going out fishing" or whatever it may be. Then unfortunately, because we are not usually listening, we come back the next day or Monday and say what did you do this past weekend. That tells them that you did not listen to them, or you did not care when you asked them previously, so why should they even tell you going forward?

Let's look at it another way. When they tell you that's it's their daughter's fifth birthday on Saturday, you now know the date, how old she is, and how they are going to celebrate it. Program that into your phone, enter into your calendar that is Phillip's daughter's birthday on March 23rd. Set that as a reminder to remind you one day prior every year going forward. Then next year you can go out and say, "It is Tanya's birthday this weekend, what are you all doing for her birthday?" Talk about connections, you just made a connection with that person that will last into eternity.

Now think about doing that with everyone, how long does it really take to stop and ask how your day is going, what are you doing this weekend, what did you do this past weekend? They will give you the info, now do something with it. People ask me all the time how I remember all this stuff. The reality is I do not, but if it is important to them, then it is important to me. So, I take the extra moment to program it in a place that will tell me automatically what is going on and who I need to see.

Let's shift to rapport building for a moment. The significance of rapport building is a crucial foundation for fostering meaningful connections within our team. Building rapport goes beyond the confines of the workplace, it's about finding common ground and shared experiences that transcend the personal and professional realm.

For instance, I vividly recall a moment when I discovered that a fellow team member and I both had children playing high school lacrosse. This connection point became a powerful catalyst for rapport building. We eagerly shared stories of our children's triumphs and challenges on the field, finding common ground and forging a deeper bond. This simple connection served as a reminder that beneath our professional roles, we are individuals with lives outside of work, brimming with shared experiences that can create lasting memories. By actively seeking out these connection points, we foster an environment where team members can understand and support one another, building the foundation for enduring memories and a strong sense of camaraderie.

Here's how to create another one-minute memory. Most of these ideas will be hidden in plain sight. They hide inside of other normal day-to-day activities. With intentionality, they can be created when you see someone doing something that you know could be completed much easier or in a more effective and efficient way that would be less taxing on them. When you see this, take a moment to help them with it. Now you are making a connection that shows them that you genuinely care about them and their ability to do the task at hand. So, I challenge you to go out and create some memories but do not expect them to come back overnight. You are laying the foundation for things to come back in the future because we are creating moments in time.

Creating these moments is extremely impactful to our people, but you must do this expecting nothing in return. As soon as you expect something in return, it is very apparent that you are just going through the motions and not trying to learn them for who they are.

As we conclude this chapter on memories, let's carry with us the realization that leadership is not solely about achieving goals or driving results, but about the lives we touch and the memories we leave in our wake. Each interaction, each conversation, and each act of genuine care has the potential to create lasting impressions. Let us commit ourselves to being intentional, empathetic, and attentive leaders who strive to create memories that inspire, uplift, and ignite the flame of greatness within our teams. May our legacy be remembered not only for the tasks accomplished but for the memories we helped to create along the extraordinary journey of growth and collaboration.

"...let's carry with us the realization that leadership is not solely about achieving goals or driving results, but about the lives we touch and the memories we leave in our wake."

Reflecting on "Memories"

1. Are you creating memories in the lives of the people you interact with? How can you make intentional connections that leave a lasting impact?

_____

_____

_____

_____

_____

2. How can you demonstrate genuine care and interest in your team members' personal and professional lives? What steps can you take to learn about their goals, milestones, and celebrations to strengthen your connection with them?

_____

_____

_____

_____

_____

3. How often do you pause to assist others when you notice they could use help or guidance? How can you incorporate moments of support and assistance into your daily interactions to create meaningful connections?

_____

_____

_____

_____

_____

Notes

Chapter 10

Leveraging Strengths

In the realm of leadership, one of the fundamental responsibilities is to harness the collective talents and abilities of a team. The art of strength-based delegation, when executed effectively, can be the catalyst for both individual and organizational growth. By recognizing and leveraging the strengths of each team member, leaders can create an environment where weaknesses fade, and everyone thrives through continuous learning and development.

One of the many things I have learned over the years of leading teams and growing new leaders is that one of the hardest things for new leaders or managers to learn is how to delegate effectively. I have stated for years that weaknesses are disguised as opportunities; opportunities to grow and gain experiences both personally and professionally. In this chapter, I will use the word weakness because that is what we commonly refer to it as, but if you will open your mind to changing your thoughts from someone's weakness to someone's opportunities, then you will create the stage for unwavering growth of everyone on the team. Our team members will chase opportunities while running from their weaknesses, but in my opinion, they are usually one in the

"I have stated for years that weaknesses are disguised as opportunities; opportunities to grow and gain experiences both personally and professionally."

same.

Understanding the power of strength-based delegation considers the true power of the team. Strength-based delegation is not merely about assigning tasks or relieving oneself of their own responsibilities. It is an intentional process that requires a deep understanding of the team's capabilities, strengths, and weaknesses. When leaders pair the right individuals together, they create a dynamic synergy where each person's strengths complement the weaknesses or opportunities of others.

By delegating tasks to individuals who excel in these areas, leaders not only ensure the work is completed effectively and efficiently but also provide an opportunity for personal and professional growth. It is through this deliberate pairing that team members learn from one another, pushing each other to reach new heights and overcome their perceived limitations.

When we, as leaders, delegate tasks with the aim of building upon our team's strengths, something remarkable happens. The weaknesses that once hindered progress begin to fade. By focusing on what individuals excel at, leaders create an environment that fosters confidence, collaboration, and innovation.

It is also worth noting that we, as humans, usually try to avoid our weaknesses. When our team members avoid their weaknesses, we latch on and constantly counsel them about what they are not doing. We lose sight of what they are doing effectively. This is a key component of unwelcome turnover. When we only focus on what our team members are not doing so well, we get locked in on it and think to ourselves, "I am going to have to make a decision here, they are just not getting it." Or the team member gets tired of the pressure knowing that they are contributing heavily in other areas, so they then shift to start looking for their next place of employment. Either way, we are setting ourselves up to lose the talent that we have spent so much time developing and connecting with. At times, it will be necessary to make personnel changes, but let's make sure it is not because we did not capitalize on their strengths effectively and push them away for the wrong reasons.

Let's build the atmosphere around them that complements their strengths, which puts them in position to be supported so we can help them minimize their weaknesses. When we do this, our team members feel more fulfilled, all while becoming more confident, efficient, and effective in their respected roles.

For instance, imagine a team consisting of individuals with diverse skill sets. Instead of fixating on their weaknesses, a wise leader would assign tasks that align with their strengths. The strategist is given projects that require critical thinking and analysis, while the communicator is entrusted with client interactions. As a result, each team member is empowered to contribute meaningfully, amplifying the team's overall performance.

To foster continuous personal and professional growth we must delegate with intentionality. When done with intentionality, it sets the stage for continuous growth. When team members are paired based on their strengths, they not only excel in their assigned tasks but also have the platform to learn from each other. For example, the strategist might acquire valuable communication skills from the communicator, while the communicator might develop a strategic mindset.

Furthermore, the process of delegation encourages individuals to step out of their comfort zones. By taking on tasks that challenge their existing capabilities, team members expand their horizons and acquire new skills. This not only benefits them personally but also enriches the team's collective expertise.

As a leader, it is imperative to approach delegation with thoughtfulness and intentionality. The leader's role is to identify the strengths of each team member and align them with tasks that allow those strengths to shine. Effective leaders possess the ability to discern the unique talents and abilities of their team and assign responsibilities accordingly. As this happens, sometimes the job roles will need to be modified to best fit the team member, instead of making the team member take on elements that do not align with their strengths. This is commonly referred to as putting everyone in the right seat on the bus. Taking a similar approach, sometimes we must create or design the right seat that best complements the individual's strengths, rather than putting them in a seat that somewhat fits. Meaning, create the job role that best fits their strengths to get the best performance, while building their confidence along the way.

Additionally, leaders should foster an environment that encourages open communication and collaboration. By creating a safe space where team members can freely share their ideas, challenges, and successes, leaders enable mutual learning and growth. Leaders should also be readily available to provide guidance, support, and constructive feedback, nurturing the development of their team members.

Remember, effective strength-based delegation is not about simply pushing tasks down the hierarchy to get tasks off our desks. It is about making meaningful connections, and learning the strengths of each team member, then delegating with intentionality.

As leaders, we have an obligation to recognize and cultivate the unique strengths within our teams. By assigning tasks that align with those strengths, we unlock the full potential of our team members, allowing them to excel and contribute at their highest level. In doing so, we pave the way for their continuous growth, building a culture of collaboration, innovation, and mutual support.

Strength-based delegation is a powerful tool for leadership. By pairing the right teams together and creating, building, or modifying the job roles to leverage the individual strengths, leaders can create an environment where weaknesses become inconsequential. Through intentional delegation, team members learn from one another, pushing each other to reach new heights and continuously grow both personally and professionally.

"As leaders, we have an obligation to recognize and cultivate the unique strengths within our teams."

Reflecting on "Leveraging Strengths"

1. How can you shift your perspective from viewing weaknesses as obstacles to embracing them as opportunities for growth, both for yourself and your team members?

_____

_____

_____

_____

_____

2. Are you delegating tasks based on the strengths and capabilities of your team members? How can you ensure that the tasks assigned align with their strengths to foster personal and professional growth?

_____

_____

_____

_____

_____

3. In what ways can you create an environment that encourages open communication and collaboration among team members? How can you actively support their development through guidance, support, and constructive feedback?

_____

_____

_____

_____

_____

Notes

Chapter 11

Hire to Compliment

I intentionally left writing about hiring and onboarding until one of the later chapters because I genuinely want you to focus on what you can accomplish by connecting and engaging with your current team members. However, with growth, promotions, innovations, expansions, and other opportunities that arise, you will need to hire and onboard the right candidates to compliment the team. Notice I said compliment the team. If we are hiring the right candidates, and onboarding them properly, they will complement the team right out of the gate.

As our organization grows, innovates, and evolves, hiring and onboarding the right individuals becomes crucial for maintaining a strong and productive workforce. While effective leadership can minimize employee turnover through proper direction, guidance, and development, there are several instances where new hires are necessary. My focus here is to help you make the best possible hiring decisions rather than convenient ones. This chapter explores the significance of good hiring and onboarding practices and provides you the info needed to create a comprehensive guideline to help you and your team make informed decisions on who, how and when to bring in additional team members to onboard and develop. By creating some guidelines and practices, you can ensure your organization continues to thrive, meet, and even exceed its objectives.

Unfortunately, we often do not look for a new team member using any type of guideline. We place an ad, pick a few of the applicants that responded, and hope that if we hire one or two of them that they will work out. In all honesty, we are setting them up for failure right out of the gate. Occasionally we stumble across a rockstar, so we continue to do it the same way each time. Then when they start, we are not prepared to onboard them effectively, so they have a mountain to climb right out of the gate.

Let's take a different approach. But first I will tell you what has worked for me and the organizations I have been a part of along my leadership journey. We have used the guidelines of the three C's: Character, Competency and Chemistry.

Character: Assessing character helps determine whether a candidate's values, ethics, and integrity align with the organization's culture and goals. I want to know if this is someone that I want to represent our organization both internally and externally. This becomes a judgement call, but by asking the right questions you will be amazed at how much you can learn about how someone is wired.

Competency: Focusing on this word alone, it is a bit misleading within our organization. From the surface, it sounds like I want to know if they can hit the ground running with a certain skill set. However, I am really trying to figure out if they are a team player, if they are coachable, and willing to try something new. At times, they may even bring a different approach to something they may have learned previously. It is important for them to be willing to share this with their new team and team members as well. Yes, I want to hire extraordinary talent, but it is also important to our organization for them to be developable along with being open to innovative ideas, and methods along the way.

Chemistry: This refers to the interpersonal dynamics and compatibility between team members. A good team fit can contribute to collaboration, cooperation, and a positive work atmosphere. This requires us to put some thought into where they can fit in, and who they will be working with. If we are making informed hiring decisions, we will know if they will be willing to try innovative ideas and approaches, willing to work together as a team, and if they bring something that compliments the team in some way right out of the gate.

Having these guidelines, I can ask my department heads and hiring managers why they chose who they chose. I want to know why they chose this candidate, and why this candidate chose us. I do not do this to control any part of the hiring process. I do this so that my department heads and hiring managers put thought into why they are making this choice, rather than just making the convenient choice. Additionally, asking the candidate why they are choosing us lets them know that we want to be who and what they are looking for. It also gives us as an organization a connection point to create some initial conversations as they onboard with us. Asking the candidate this question gives us valuable information as to how well they fit the three C's.

I am not here to give you any certain guidelines to follow. I want you to create your own. It is extremely important that you have some type of expectations set for those you are looking to uphold the vision and values of your organization. Then set the expectations and guidelines around it. Create a guide of at least three traits you want in the right candidate. Then when you or your team interviews them, they have something to go by. The candidate does not always need to have the traits out of the gate, but they do need to be developable. For example, if you need to hire someone that constantly communicates with customers, the ideal candidate is not someone that wants to stay behind the scenes.

I know this all sounds very elementary, but in most cases we all hire someone, and sometimes anyone, to fill a void because we feel like we just need someone immediately. Slowing down the hiring process will allow you to think through the role at hand. Then you will start to process who can do that role, and the subsequent roles that could follow. Then, almost magically, the right candidate surfaces or at least comes to mind. You may ask, how does this make the next right candidate surface? This happens mostly because we start thinking about the team members we currently have as well as the candidates that we previously interviewed.

As we process through this, we usually land on our next team member. Then the subsequent conversations are totally different, and we start painting the metaphoric picture in their mind on how and where they will fit in and contribute to the team right out of the gate. Now, instead of hoping they say yes, we are building their confidence for the role they have not even accepted yet. If this is done effectively, by the end of the interview, they cannot see themselves doing anything else other than the opportunity in front of them. This allows the conversation to shift to thinking about when they will start, instead of considering if they will take on the challenge.

It is time to shift to effective onboarding. Now that we have the right candidate in mind and they have given you their commitment, let's start preparing for day one. All too often, when we land on a great hire, on day one they end up questioning themselves if they made the right decision coming on board with our organization. This is common, but it is certainly preventable. We have made the decision to give this person an opportunity to join our team. Let's make sure we are as prepared for them as possible. Set a time to do all the pre-hire requirements prior to day one. Have all their needed access and logins set, business cards, name tags, email addresses, and have a process to introduce them to the entire team on day one. Be sure to have the conversation about dress code or have their attire ready for them beforehand, because it is equally important that they look like they are part of the team on day one.

This again may sound elementary, but far too often, our onboarding is reactionary, and reacting to our new team members on their first day will erode the confidence they had in the beginning with this being the right place for them. Afterall, we want them to tell their previous colleagues that they made a great decision, and they should consider it as well. When we do this, and follow the other elements outlined in this book, we will have a list of candidates waiting and knocking at our door to get a chance to be a part of an effective team, and organization.

Afterall, good hiring practices are the cornerstone of sustainable development, growth, and success in any organization. By creating a guideline and incorporating it into standard practice, both you and your team can and will make well-informed decisions that align with the organization's vision, values, and objectives.

Remember, while evaluating candidates based on the criteria's you choose, it is essential to strike a balance between each of them. Prioritizing one criterion over others could lead to a lopsided team dynamic. In the example I gave, assessing character, chemistry, and competency collectively will increase the likelihood of finding the right fit for your team and foster a culture of collaboration, growth, and success.

Building a solid foundation through effective hiring and onboarding not only enables the acquisition of top talent but also contributes to fostering a positive work environment, enhancing team performance, and fueling continuous development, all while making you the employer of choice. With these practices in place, you can confidently navigate the hiring and onboarding process, bringing in individuals who will thrive within the organization and contribute to its long-term success. Tying all this together with effective buy-in, collaboration, and execution, allows you and your team to build a lasting dynasty within your organization.

"Afterall, good hiring practices are the cornerstone of sustainable development, growth, and success in any organization."

Reflecting on "Hire to Compliment"

1. How can you shift your approach to hiring from reactive and convenient decisions to making well-informed choices that align with your organization's vision and values?

_____

_____

_____

_____

_____

2. What steps can you take to improve your onboarding process and ensure that new team members feel welcomed, supported, and confident in their decision to join your organization?

_____

_____

_____

_____

_____

3. In what ways can you proactively prepare for the onboarding process before a new team member's first day? How can you ensure that they have a smooth transition and feel valued and appreciated from the start?

_____

_____

_____

_____

_____

Notes

Chapter 12

Team Building

Effective team building lies at the heart of exceptional leadership. It is not merely about assembling a group of individuals but rather crafting a cohesive unit that thrives on collaboration, constructive interaction, and mutual support. In this chapter, we delve into the transformative power of team building, where each team member's strengths are harnessed to complement one another's weaknesses and seize opportunities. Moreover, we explore the vital role of building the bench, preparing team members for their future roles, and cultivating a culture of growth and development. By investing in team building, leaders create a foundation for success, unlocking the full potential of their teams and fostering an environment where individuals flourish, challenges are devoured, and collective achievement becomes the norm.

Building may not even be the right word, because we are never done building our teams. It is an ongoing endless journey. It is our responsibility to assemble the right team with people that can effectively collaborate all while building each other up and focusing on each of their individual strengths. In an earlier chapter we talked about the impact that comes from identifying each of our team members' strengths. We usually talk about our team's weaknesses more than we talk about their strengths. When we do this, we are constantly reminding them what they are not good at, and this decreases their level of confidence, which in turn decreases their overall productivity.

I have learned from my experience that delegation, when utilized effectively, can be a powerful tool in leadership, particularly in leveraging the strengths of team members. A skilled leader understands that they cannot achieve success single-handedly and that their team possesses a diverse range of talents and capabilities. By delegating tasks and responsibilities to individuals whose strengths align with the requirements, leaders can tap into their team's full potential. This approach not only maximizes productivity but also fosters a sense of ownership and empowerment among team members.

Effective delegation involves careful consideration of each team member's skills, expertise, and interests. It requires clear communication of objectives, expectations, and desired outcomes. By aligning tasks with the strengths of individuals, leaders enable their team members to thrive, unleash their creativity, and deliver exceptional results. Moreover, delegation demonstrates trust and confidence in the abilities of team members, encouraging them to take on new challenges, grow professionally, and develop their own leadership skills. Ultimately, effective delegation empowers the team, allowing them to collectively leverage their strengths, collaborate efficiently, and achieve outstanding results.

I am often asked, "How do you find all these team members that fit in and work so well together?" The truth is, they are the same people that have been fired, or quit their previous employer. In most cases, these are the people that have some areas of opportunity (weaknesses), but the previous employer only focused on their weaknesses, and constantly counseled them instead of coaching them to get better at what they were struggling with. This usually continues until they fire them, or they leave on their own. In reality, this particular person was performing exceptionally well in five or six other areas, but their previous manager only focused on their mistakes or weaknesses.

Now, after going through our hiring process, and onboarding, we connect with them in ways to understand their strengths and opportunities. With this, we put them on a team that needs their strengths, while keeping their opportunities in mind. The team they land on now compliments each other with opposing strengths and opportunities. This is effective team building, all while putting each team member in a position for them to work with someone that can help them continue to grow and develop.

Let us look at it from another angle for a moment. Our teams are made up of other humans, and humans need and want recognition to perform at their best. If we focus on their strengths, and constantly remind them of their strengths, they know that we are paying attention to them. More importantly we are paying attention to what they are doing well.

When we learn what their strengths are, we can now build a team with opposing strengths. Now, rather than focusing on the things they do not do as well yet, you are putting people around them that complement their areas of opportunities. Yes, remember they are opportunities, not weaknesses. When we tell them they are not good at something, they will naturally try to avoid it, but if we coach them through their opportunities, they will usually embrace them.

Now we are starting to learn more about our team members. If we have someone that constantly runs from their opportunities but performs well while working in areas that compliments their strengths, then we have someone that is comfortable doing what they are doing for some time. This is not necessarily the one that should take on more responsibilities at this moment in time. This may change over time as they become more confident in their current role, and the roles in front of them.

On the other hand, if we have someone that wants to work on their opportunities, as well as perform at the things they excel at, we are now building someone that is versatile. As they become more versatile, they are preparing themselves for the next role in front of them.

You are now building the bench. Building the bench is extremely important for your growth as well because we cannot move forward professionally if we do not have someone to back-fill us almost seamlessly.

Let me address the monster in the room. Often, we limit our team's growth because we do not want them to be able to do our jobs, mostly because we fear they may replace us. If this is you, you must let this go, because you are holding yourself back, all while holding everyone on your team back, too.

If you are constantly building your team, you are constantly growing people that can do your job as effectively as you can. As this happens, you become less concerned about taking time off, and when you are having an off day, things are not stacking up, because your team is picking up the pieces. As we combine the elements outlined in the previous chapters, we now, almost seamlessly, are building a collaborative team from the intentionality of building an effective team.

Effective team building stands as a cornerstone of exceptional

"Often, we limit our team's growth because we do not want them to be able to do our jobs, mostly because we fear they may replace us."

leadership. It is the art of harnessing each team member's strengths, allowing them to complement one another's weaknesses and seize opportunities collectively. By building the bench and preparing team members for future roles, leaders foster a culture of growth, development, and continuous learning. The importance of team building cannot be overstated, as it paves the way for collaboration, constructive interaction, and the achievement of extraordinary results. As leaders, let's prioritize team building as an essential element of our leadership journey, and witness the effective transformations that unfold when we foster an environment where each team member can thrive and collectively reach new heights of success. As these elements blend harmoniously, infused with a touch of innovation, your team and organization will consistently achieve industry-leading results that will be coveted by all.

"As these elements blend harmoniously, infused with a touch of innovation, your team and organization will consistently achieve industry-leading results that will be coveted by all."

Reflecting on "Team Building"

1. How can you shift your focus from emphasizing weaknesses to recognizing and leveraging the strengths of your team members? How can this approach enhance their confidence and overall productivity?

_____

_____

_____

_____

_____

2. In what ways can you effectively delegate tasks and responsibilities to align with the strengths of your team members? How can this practice maximize productivity, foster a sense of ownership, and empower your team as a whole?

_____

_____

_____

_____

_____

3. What steps can you take to build a versatile team by complementing each team member's strengths with individuals who have opposing strengths? How can this approach contribute to their professional growth and create a strong bench for future opportunities?

_____

_____

_____

_____

Notes

Chapter 13

Who Needs a Title?

I am often asked if a title is needed to be a leader. The short answer is no, anyone can be a leader in any position. In my experience, some of the most impactful leaders are those who do not hold prominent titles but possess a profound ability to inspire and influence others. These individuals stand out as leaders by embodying key qualities such as integrity, empathy, and a commitment to the team's success. They exhibit a keen sense of purpose and passion, always striving to exceed expectations and contribute beyond their immediate responsibilities. By fostering collaboration, leading by example, and actively seeking opportunities to support and mentor others, these leaders create an environment that nurtures growth, innovation, and collective achievement. Thus, the essence of leadership lies not in a title, but in the actions, mindset, and impact that an individual brings to their team and the organization as a whole. Learning to be an effective leader requires a few intentional elements that we must regularly practice no matter what position we hold.

There are two interconnected pillars that bring everything in this book together: the relentless pursuit of personal and professional growth, and the cultivation of skills within ourselves and our team members. A leader's journey is one of constant learning, evolving, and adapting to the ever-changing landscape of the world we live in. This chapter explores the significance of continuous improvement as well as the imperative role leaders play in fostering the growth and development of their team members.

Effective leadership goes beyond mere guidance and direction. Effective leadership aims to create a positive atmosphere to set the stage for positive change, foster growth both personally and professionally of each team member. Doing this sets the stage to achieve industry-leading results in any industry, all while growing and developing new up-and-coming leaders.

Effective leaders inspire and motivate their teams to reach new heights, achieve ambitious goals, and push beyond their wildest limits. They help their team understand that good is not good enough, because we must always strive and push to be better than the day before.

Leaders who embody a lifelong learning mindset demonstrate humility and an eagerness to acquire knowledge. They understand that leadership is not a destination, it is a journey. True growth lies in tackling the status quo head-on. By expanding their horizons, leaders gain valuable insights, cultivate a broader perspective, and develop the ability to anticipate trends and changes in their respective industries. Their commitment to continuous learning sets a powerful example for their team members, encouraging a culture of curiosity and self-improvement within the organization.

Lifelong learning is not limited to gaining technical knowledge. It encompasses the development of skills such as emotional intelligence, communication, and critical thinking. Leaders who embrace personal and professional growth enhance their ability to connect with others, motivate their teams, and foster a collaborative environment. By honing these skills, leaders can resolve conflicts, and inspire others to achieve their full potential. Through constant self-reflection and improvement, leaders, with the power of their teams, become more adaptable and resilient, capable of navigating the complexities of an ever-evolving environment.

Understanding generational differences is a vital aspect that should not be underestimated. Each generation brings with it a unique set of values, experiences, and perspectives shaped by the era in which they grew up. Recognizing and appreciating these diverse perspectives can foster stronger relationships, enhance collaboration, and drive innovation within teams and organizations. By acknowledging and accepting generational differences, leaders can tailor their communication styles, motivational strategies, and work environments to accommodate the needs and aspirations of individuals from different age groups. This not only promotes inclusivity and engagement but also harnesses the collective power of multi-generational teams, increased job fulfilment while leading to increased creativity, productivity, and organizational success.

Instead of fixating on the flaws of various generations, whether current, upcoming, or retiring, it is essential to identify what truly motivates them. Each generation starts with its own unique foundation, leading to distinct reactions to different situations. Through my firsthand experiences, I have discovered that by establishing genuine connections with individuals from different generations, regardless of disparities, we can gain insights into their driving forces and sources of inspiration. For example, baby boomers tend to remain committed to a single job until retirement, and if they have the energy, they might even embark on a second career before retiring again. On the other hand, some of the younger generations are constantly seeking new approaches and endeavors, necessitating the provision of alternative paths for them to explore and pursue.

While leaders are committed to their own growth, they recognize the value in developing the skills and potential of their team members. Effective leaders understand that their success is fundamentally tied to the success of their team. By investing in their team's growth, leaders create an environment that nurtures talent, fosters creativity, and maximizes productivity.

Developing team members goes beyond providing training programs or workshops. It involves understanding the unique strengths and aspirations of each individual and empowering them to unleash their full potential. Leaders who actively mentor and coach their team members create a sense of trust, loyalty, and commitment. By delegating meaningful tasks and offering constructive feedback, leaders foster a growth mindset within their team, promoting personal and professional development.

The development of team members not only benefits the individuals themselves, but also contributes to the long-term success of the organization. By developing their team members with the necessary skills and knowledge, leaders create a robust and adaptable workforce capable of tackling almost any challenge head-on. Additionally, leaders who actively foster a culture of learning and development attract and retain top talent, as individuals are drawn to leaders and organizations that invest in their growth and provide opportunities for advancement. By prioritizing the development of team members, leaders create a self-sustaining cycle of growth and excellence.

An effective leader is someone who understands the

"Additionally, leaders who actively foster a culture of learning and development attract and retain top talent, as individuals are drawn to leaders and organizations that invest in their growth and provide opportunities for advancement."

importance of empathy, communication, and collaboration. They possess a set of essential qualities that enable them to inspire and lead their team effectively. These qualities include, but not limited to:

Empathy: Effective leaders understand the needs, concerns, and aspirations of their team members. They listen actively, empathize with their struggles, and create an environment of trust, safety, and support.

Communication: Effective leaders are skilled communicators who can articulate their vision, expectations, and can give feedback clearly and effectively. They communicate frequently, honestly, and with respect, and actively seek feedback from all their team members.

Active Listening: Active listening seeks to understand what is being said, rather than listening to respond. Effective leaders listen intently to the needs and thoughts of each of their team members. Active listening helps them build trust and helps them understand their team members' situations and feelings, with the goal for the team member to feel heard and understood.

Responsible: Effective leaders hold themselves and their team members responsible and accountable for their actions and decisions. They take ownership of their mistakes as well as the mistakes of their team members. They learn from them, and strive to continuously improve their performance.

Collaboration: Effective leaders foster collaboration, creativity, and innovation by encouraging their team members to work together, share ideas, and learn from each other. They recognize the value of diversity and inclusivity and create a space where everyone feels welcome, respected, and encouraged to express their ideas.

Vision: Effective leaders have an unobstructed vision of what they want to achieve and the path they need to take to get there. They commonly are methodical thinkers who can anticipate challenges, evaluate risks, and make informed decisions that align with their long-term goals. They see things differently than they are and challenge the status quo.

The journey towards greatness never ceases. Leaders who embrace lifelong learning and invest in the development of their team members unlock a world of possibilities. Effective leadership is about more than just creating and attacking the next *Mile One*, building teams, giving orders, and delegating tasks. It requires you to be committed to ongoing learning while transferring that newly learned knowledge to each member of the team. It requires a combination of these essential qualities that enable leaders to inspire, motivate, develop, and guide their team towards success. By understanding and embodying these qualities, leaders with or without a title can create a positive, productive, and fulfilling work environment that benefits everyone involved, as well as the organization. As a result, by investing in their team's growth, leaders build a cohesive unit capable of achieving industry leading results.

"The journey towards greatness never ceases."

Reflecting on "Who Needs a Title?"

1. Reflect on your own leadership journey and the impact of titles on leadership. Have you witnessed or experienced leaders who did not hold prominent titles but still had a profound ability to inspire and influence others? How did they embody key qualities such as integrity, empathy, and commitment to the team's success? How can you apply these qualities in your own leadership approach, regardless of your title or position?

_____

_____

_____

_____

_____

2. Consider the two interconnected pillars mentioned in the chapter: personal and professional growth, and the cultivation of skills within yourself and your team members. How have you pursued continuous improvement in your own journey as a leader? What strategies have you used to foster the growth and development of your team members? Are there any specific areas where you can enhance your commitment to lifelong learning and skill development?

_____

_____

_____

_____

_____

3. Reflect on the importance of understanding generational differences in leadership. How have you navigated and appreciated the unique perspectives and values brought by

different generations within your team? Have you tailored your communication styles, motivational strategies, and work environments to accommodate the needs and aspirations of individuals from different age groups? How can you further leverage generational diversity to drive innovation, collaboration, and organizational success?

_____

_____

_____

_____

_____

Notes

Chapter 14

Tying It All Together

One of the greatest leaders of our time is Alan Mulally. During his time at Boeing, he faced challenges. One was sifting through the wake of disruption caused from the terrorist attacks on September 11, 2001. Another was taking on the challenges of saving Ford Motor Company in late 2006 only to be amplified by the recession looming around the corner. Amplified yet again by the freezing of the American financial system, and the other two American rivals needing a bail out to stay afloat, then both rivals ultimately filing bankruptcy in 2009 to put them on track to have a chance of survival.

Alan and Ford Motor Company decided to go alone, and not take taxpayers money to stay afloat. He had already started doing some much-needed restructuring and was making the necessary changes to further develop a One Ford plan he created in his early days at Ford, giving Ford a chance to go through the toughest financial crisis we have seen in our time without taking taxpayers' money. Alan did this by making changes that were needed to save Ford and create an exciting, viable, sustainable, and profitably growing Ford for the future.

In my experience, most leaders resist making the needed changes in our organizations because we are afraid to challenge the way we have always done things. We fear what could go wrong, rather than driving towards what could go right. This, perhaps, is one of the biggest problems within our personal and professional lives.

As I wrote this book, I considered writing a chapter about change management based on the feedback I got from one of my early readers, Tony Frankenberger. I did not want the reader to lose sight of the impact that the power of collaboration of everyone on the team along with positive influence could truly do for their team, organization, and their personal lives. I also could not let go of one of the biggest challenges that faces most leaders today. That challenge is the ability to navigate and manage change in a positive and productive way.

As I closed in on the finish line of this book, I reached out to Alan Mulally to ask him for an endorsement as he has been an unknowing mentor of mine for almost two decades. I knew the way he led at both Boeing and Ford Motor Company. He again unknowingly provided me with validation for the way in which I tried to lead the teams I work with. When we connected, we chatted for a bit to get to know each other in person. He said, "Send me a note with the book," and if it aligned with his style of servant leadership (which I believe to be the only form of leadership) he would consider endorsing *Mile One*.

The note:
Dear Mr. Mulally,

I cannot express how honored and grateful I am to have the opportunity to reach out to you, someone who has been an unwitting but profound mentor in my life. Over the years, I have followed your remarkable journey and admired your exceptional leadership at Ford Motor Company, and your approach has deeply resonated with me as I lead Bozard Ford Lincoln.

I just completed writing a book titled *Mile One, an Endless Journey to Effective Leadership*, which encapsulates the insights and lessons I've learned from observing your leadership style and applying it to my own professional and personal life. Your impact on Ford's revival and your emphasis on teamwork, transparency, and relentless optimism have served as a guiding light for me in steering our dealerships towards success and fostering a culture of collaboration and growth.

It would be an absolute dream come true and an immeasurable honor if you would consider endorsing my book. Your backing would undoubtedly provide credibility and encouragement to readers and aspiring leaders looking to make a difference in their respective fields.

Knowing the busy and demanding schedule you maintain; I understand that your time is precious. I have attached the manuscript of *Mile One, an Endless Journey to Effective Leadership* to this email. Please peruse it at your convenience. I truly believe that your support would amplify its impact on aspiring leaders, encouraging them to adopt effective leadership strategies that can drive transformation and success in their organizations.

I cannot emphasize enough how influential your legacy has been on my journey. Receiving your endorsement would be a defining moment in my life. Your wisdom, humility, and genuine passion for leadership have inspired me, and I hope that by sharing my experiences in this book, I can help others benefit from your valuable insights as well.

Thank you for considering my request. Your support would help fuel my determination to continue making a positive difference in the world of leadership.

With utmost respect and admiration,

Ed Roberts

COO Bozard Ford Lincoln

Alan and I connected a few times by phone and zoom to go over his thoughts on the book. He said to me, "Your book certainly aligns with my approach to leadership and I feel that the world that we live in today could use some help with how to manage change in a positive and productive way." He said "I'll be pleased to support you with a chapter about expecting and managing change in a positive way, because it would tie all your "Working Together" points together." So, you as the reader of *Mile One, an Endless Journey to Effective Leadership* are getting a bonus from me and one of the greatest leaders of our time. Please note there are some thought provoking references about Alan's "Working Together" Leadership and Management System at the end of this chapter.

One of the key insights he shared about his "Working Together" Leadership and Management system was the importance of having a compelling vision, a comprehensive strategy, and positive relentless implementation plan called the weekly Business Plan Review (BPR) meetings. The BPR was pivotal in driving collaboration and managing change in a positive way. The BPR included all of the leadership team that also represented all of the stakeholders. During these BPR meetings, Alan and the leadership team utilized a simple yet powerful color-based system of red, yellow, and green assessments of their contribution plan status to highlight opportunities and challenges in their area of responsibility and the organization. Red items were welcomed "GEMS" that indicated areas that required immediate attention. Yellow items represented concerns that needed monitoring, and green items signified progress and achievements. This color-coded approach not only fostered transparency but also enabled teams to rally together, tackle issues collectively, and celebrate successes. By creating a safe culture of open communication, transparency, and accountability, Alan's BPR meetings transformed the way change was perceived and executed, resulting in remarkable turnarounds at both companies.

Change is an inevitable part of life and business, and nowhere is it more apparent than in the realm of leadership. The ability to effectively manage change is a hallmark of great leaders who not only adapt to new circumstances but also inspire their teams to embrace, enjoy and thrive through transformation. In this chapter, we explore the profound significance of change management and its role in the journey of leadership.

Change, often accompanied by uncertainty and resistance, can be a daunting prospect for individuals and organizations alike. Yet, commonly, it is through change that growth and progress are achieved. As a leader, your role in change management is paramount. You must function as the guiding force, instilling a sense of purpose, and empowering your team to navigate uncharted territories with confidence and resilience.

One of the first steps in effective change management is creating a compelling vision that inspires and motivates. This vision serves as a beacon, guiding your team towards the desired future vision. By clearly articulating the benefits and opportunities that lie ahead, you can help alleviate the apprehensions and fears associated with change.

"The ability to effectively manage change is a hallmark of great leaders who not only adapt to new circumstances but also inspire their teams to embrace, enjoy and thrive through transformation."

Communicating the vision consistently and passionately ensures that everyone understands the rationale behind the transformation and can see the value in embracing it.

Along the journey of change, resistance is bound to arise. People naturally gravitate towards familiarity and the proven routine, making it challenging to break free from the comfort of the status quo. As a leader, it is crucial to acknowledge and address resistance with empathy and patience. Open communication and actively listening to concerns can help uncover the underlying reasons for resistance, allowing you to address them effectively. By involving your team in the change process and empowering them to contribute ideas and solutions, you foster a sense of ownership and commitment that paves the way for smoother transitions.

Change also necessitates the cultivation of learning and growth mindsets within your team. Encourage an environment where "GEMS" are seen as valuable learning opportunities rather than failures. Emphasize continuous improvement and provide the necessary resources and support to facilitate growth and development. As a leader, you set the example by expecting and encouraging feedback, adapting your own approach, and demonstrating resilience in the face of setbacks.

Successful change management requires a well-thought-out plan, but flexibility is equally important. Recognize that the journey may have unexpected twists and turns and be prepared to adapt your strategies accordingly. Agile leadership, marked by the ability to pivot and make informed decisions in real-time, is essential to navigate the ever-evolving landscape of change.

In this closing chapter of *Mile One, an Endless Journey to Effective Leadership*, my conversation with Alan Mulally about

"Change also necessitates the cultivation of learning and growth mindsets within your team."

change management and managing change in a positive way emphasized the importance of transparency, communication, and teamwork in fostering a culture of adaptability. Alan's experience at Boeing and Ford Motor Company demonstrated that change, though often daunting, could be effectively navigated by embracing challenges as opportunities and fostering an environment where individuals at all levels felt empowered to contribute to the organization's success.

By implementing the red, yellow, and green system, Alan exemplified how simple, yet powerful tools can create clarity, promote collaboration, and inspire leaders to remain focused on achieving their shared goals. As you embark on your own endless journey, let's remember that true transformation comes not merely from the actions of one individual, but from the collective efforts of a team united in their commitment to growth, innovation, and effective leadership to create value for all the stakeholders and the greater good. Through such collaboration and dedication to positive change, we can all create a lasting impact on our organizations and the world beyond.

"Alan's experience at Boeing and Ford Motor Company demonstrated that change, though often daunting, could be effectively navigated by embracing challenges as opportunities and fostering an environment where individuals at all levels felt empowered to contribute to the organization's success."

Reflecting on "Tying It All Together"

1. Reflect on your own approach to change management: How do you typically manage change in your personal and professional life? Are you more inclined to resist change due to fear of the unknown, or do you embrace it as an opportunity for growth and progress? Consider the impact of your attitude towards change on your team and organization, and how you can cultivate a more positive and adaptive mindset.

_____

_____

_____

_____

_____

2. Consider the importance of fostering a learning mindset within your team or organization. How do you currently approach mistakes and setbacks? Are they seen as failures, or do you encourage a culture where mistakes are viewed as valuable learning opportunities? Reflect on ways you can promote continuous improvement and support your team members' development through change.

_____

_____

_____

_____

_____

Notes

Alan Mulally's "Working Together" Leadership and Management System Reference Material

https://www.amazon.com/American-Icon-Mulally-Fight-Company/dp/0307886069/ref=sr_1_1?crid=2RN7J6QS20V3&keywords=american+icon&qid=1657901304&s=books&sprefix=american+icon%2Cstripbooks%2C68&sr=1-1

https://www.dropbox.com/s/23cvx2ffn4nfymw/Alan%20Mulally%20Bio.pdf?dl=0

https://www.dropbox.com/s/73tq2zuxh7avqif/Work%20Is%20Love%20Made%20Visible%20Foreword.pdf?dl=0

https://onlinelibrary.wiley.com/doi/epdf/10.1002/ltl.20628

https://www.dropbox.com/s/t5rfo9c2cl2iuy9/EPOLH%20Foreword%20%2B%20Ch7.pdf?dl=0

https://www.dropbox.com/s/5k7agvnptfnksuz/Design%20News%20RFS.pdf?dl=0

Conclusion

Reflecting on the Endless Journey to Effective Leadership

Congratulations! You have reached the end of *Mile One, An Endless Journey to Effective Leadership.* This book has taken you on a transformative expedition through the vast landscape of leadership, providing you with invaluable insights, practical strategies, and thought-provoking reflections. As you conclude this journey, take a moment to reflect on your growth and newfound understanding of what it means to be an exceptional leader.

When we take the time to truly connect with our teams, share the vision of the organization, encourage and support collaboration, shape and develop our teams, and provide them with a path, we can accomplish what we and others may have thought was not possible. I am not saying if you break everything down into manageable steps that you will become an effective leader. Breaking things down into manageable steps and acting on them will allow you and your team to see what is truly possible with a plan or path to get to the desired vision and or goal.

Becoming an effective leader is a journey that requires commitment, dedication, and continuous learning. As you have learned throughout this book, effective leadership is about more than just delegating tasks, making decisions, and setting achievable goals. It is about inspiring and guiding your team towards a shared vision, creating, and continuously cultivating a culture of trust, collaboration, all while continuously improving your skills and knowledge of not just you as the leader, but also each member of your team.

To become an effective leader, you must have a clear

understanding of your own strengths and opportunities, your values and beliefs, and your vision for what is ahead. From there, you can develop the essential qualities of effective leadership, including vision, empathy, communication, accountability, and collaboration.

Throughout this book, we have explored various aspects of leadership, from how to foster collaboration and the impact when we inspire others. We have delved into the importance of emotional intelligence, effective communication, and embracing diversity. We have discussed the significance of integrity, resilience, and adaptability in leadership. Each chapter has provided you with a new lens through which to view your leadership journey.

The reflection questions at the end of each chapter have been designed to encourage introspection, prompting you to apply the concepts and principles discussed to your own experiences and aspirations as a leader. They have invited you to delve deep into your thoughts, values, and motivations, challenging you to continuously learn, grow, and refine your leadership approach. These questions have served as catalysts for self-discovery, prompting you to question assumptions, uncover blind spots, and unlock your full potential as a leader.

But remember, the journey does not end here. Leadership is not a destination to be reached but a perpetual expedition to be embraced. It is an ongoing process of self-improvement, learning from failures, and adapting to new challenges. I wanted to highlight exceptional leaders, with or without a title are ongoing learners. I wanted you to discover how to build upon your leadership journey, overcome obstacles, and the need to continue to evolve as a leader.

Leadership is not just about personal success, it is about making a positive impact on others and creating lasting change. The true measure of your leadership lies in the lives you touch, the inspiration you provide, and the growth you cultivate in those around you. Your journey has equipped you with the tools, insights, and mindset necessary to have influence and empower others to reach their full potential.

As you move forward on your leadership journey, keep these key lessons in mind. Be adaptable, as the world of leadership is constantly evolving. Seek feedback and continuously learn from those you lead. Embrace diversity and inclusivity, fostering an environment that celebrates the strengths and perspectives of every individual. Lead with integrity, authenticity, and empathy, inspiring trust, and loyalty among your team.

Never underestimate the impact of small steps taken consistently. Every milestone, no matter how small, brings you closer to becoming the leader you aspire to be. Remember that leadership is not about having all the answers, but about asking the right questions and empowering others to contribute their unique insights and talents.

As you conclude this book, reflect on how far you have come and the incredible potential that lies within you. Embrace the endless journey of leadership with open arms, knowing that each step you take will contribute to your growth and the positive influence you have on others.

Thank you for joining us on this transformative voyage. May *Mile One: An Endless Journey to Effective Leadership* serve as a guide, a companion, and a source of inspiration as you continue to navigate the vast landscapes of leadership. Embrace the challenges, celebrate the victories, and never stop exploring the boundless potential that lies within you.

Safe travels on your leadership journey, and may your impact be profound and everlasting.

About the Author

Ed Roberts is a seasoned leader in the automotive industry, renowned for his relentless pursuit of excellence and his passion for challenging the status quo. Born and raised in the challenging Springfield neighborhood of downtown Jacksonville, Florida, Ed's journey from humble beginnings to becoming the Chief Operations Officer at Bozard Ford Lincoln is a testament to his unwavering determination and perseverance.

Ed's career commenced in July 1992 as an apprentice technician. Since then, he has held various positions that have shaped his expertise and leadership acumen. From his early days as an apprentice to his current role as COO, Ed's unwavering commitment to personal and professional growth has propelled him forward, enabling him to make a lasting impact on the lives of those he encounters.

Throughout his over 30-year tenure in the automotive industry, Ed has dedicated himself to the development, promotion, and empowerment of individuals and teams. His innovative thinking, coupled with his ability to challenge conventional wisdom, has earned him recognition and accolades within the industry. Ed has been featured in prestigious publications like *Fixed Ops Magazine*, and he was honored as one of the *Automotive News* 30 Allstars for 2020.

Ed's expertise extends beyond the automotive realm, as he possesses a deep understanding of leadership, teamwork, overcoming adversity, embracing change, maintaining mental agility, and demonstrating perseverance. He takes tremendous pride in sharing his knowledge and experiences with others, serving as a sought-after speaker, coach, mentor, and innovator. Ed's passion for leadership and his unwavering commitment to making a difference have earned him the respect and admiration of his peers.

In his book, *Mile One: An Endless Journey to Effective Leadership*, Ed Roberts shares his profound insights and practical strategies that will elevate your leadership skills to new heights. He firmly believes that leadership is not a destination but an ongoing voyage of growth, self-discovery, and influence. Whether you are a seasoned executive, a startup founder, or an aspiring leader, *Mile One* is designed to provide valuable insights and thought-provoking reflections that will empower you to embark on your own journey to effective leadership.

Ed's life experiences and his remarkable rise from humble beginnings have shaped him into a servant leader who is deeply committed to his family and community. Beyond his professional achievements, he cherishes his role as a devoted spouse and dad, always seeking to make a positive impact on the lives of those around him.

Through *Mile One* and his continuous pursuit of excellence, Ed Roberts invites you to join him on an endless journey of growth, self-discovery, and influence. His story serves as a testament to the transformative power of determination, perseverance, and the refusal to accept mediocrity. With Ed as your guide, you will unlock the keys to effective leadership and chart your course towards personal and professional success.

Made in the USA
Columbia, SC
07 September 2023

ef8a7f22-4fbf-4607-9ae2-318a752117dfR01